Elizabethans

Elizabethans

By
A. H. Bullen

"Strong were our sires, and as they fought they writ,
Conquering with force of arms and dint of wit :
Theirs was the giant race before the flood."

DRYDEN

SECOND IMPRESSION

NEW YORK
RUSSELL & RUSSELL · INC
1962

FIRST PUBLISHED IN 1924
REISSUED 1962 BY RUSSELL & RUSSELL, INC.
L. C. CATALOG CARD NO: 62-13829

PRINTED IN THE UNITED STATES OF AMERICA

Preface

IT had been A. H. Bullen's intention to re-write and enlarge these papers and to issue them from the Press he had established at Stratford-on-Avon. So long ago as the spring of 1889 he had delivered at Oxford six lectures on English poets and dramatists, lectures that to the Oxford of that date (before his anthologies had made, of Elizabethan poetry, common knowledge), must have come almost as a revelation. It was said of him then—" He had lived among his poets : from Drayton to Campion all were his familiar friends." In after years this judgment was amply confirmed by Mr. John Masefield, writing shortly after Bullen's death : " He talked of Elizabethan books and people much as though they were alive in the streets outside, like the time come back."

The brief general introduction belongs to the old Oxford days, but the " Michael Drayton " is an amplification of an address written in 1916 and given at Stratford-on-Avon during the Shakespeare Tercentenary. Probably the " Daniel," " Chapman," and " Dekker " still stand much in their original form, but from the " Nicholas Breton " several pages are missing, pages seemingly cut away of set purpose. Their place has been filled by MS. notes, and extracts from early work now out of print, and it is hoped that this rough patchwork will be found to make a not incongruous whole. As the footnotes explain, the " Thomas Campion " is obviously untouched. Swinburne had written (16th December 1888), " I must congratulate you as cordially as I thank you. In issuing this first edition of Campion's

Preface

Works you have added a name to the roll of English poets, and one that can never be overlooked. Certainly his long neglected ghost ought now to be rejoicing in Elysium." Since then "the long neglected ghost" has taken his place among the undying ones, and Bullen's warning, in 1903, that Campion "now runs the risk of uncritical adulation" may well be repeated.

What may possibly strike the reader most in these papers is the absence of this same "uncritical adulation"; in its stead will be found what has been described as "Bullen's usual blend of complete scholarship and sound common sense." That he loved his poets none can doubt, but he loved them wisely, weighing praise or blame with an unprejudiced judgment that may astonish ears attuned to the voluble enthusiasm too often accounted as criticism. Take, for example, his verdict on Dekker, whose prose was not then as widely known as it is to-day. In 1885 Swinburne had urged upon him the claims of Marston and Dekker : "They have never been edited at all, and with all their faults they stand in the front rank of our dramatic poets." Bullen's Marston was published in 1887 ; the work wearied him and he was never satisfied with it. The Dekker was one of those many noble editions of the old dramatists, planned, discussed, dreamed over, but never brought to the birth, and the paper that stands fourth in this volume is, in essentials, a curious contrast to Swinburne's own impassioned laudation. Yet slight though it be, the measured, balanced praise gives perhaps a truer picture of that "wayward genius" and one more easily held in mind.

In April 1914 Bullen lectured before the Elizabethan Literary Society at King's College, Strand, on that curious and little known book, " A Dialogue against the Feuer Pestilence," by Dr. William

Bullein. This lecture was afterwards greatly enlarged and the parallel drawn between Bullein and Dekker should prove of interest to all careful readers. After the publication of the " Dialogue " by the Early English Text Society (1888) Swinburne wrote in congratulation to its editor, " What an admirable writer, narrator, and humorist this old namesake of yours seems to have been," and of his old namesake Bullen was justly proud. The absence of the spirit of simple jollity that makes itself felt in the songs of so many of the Elizabethans was, to him, a matter of constant regret; but it is not lacking in the prose, studded thick with quaint fancies, of the genial old doctor, while there is something of its flavour in Bullen's own writings.

The essay on Hakewill appeared in the " Nation " (New York) in 1915, and is reprinted here by the kindly courtesy of the editor. The paper on Fulke Greville, Lord Brooke, was delivered at Stratford-on-Avon in 1905 before the Shakespeare Club. " Shakespeare, The Englishman," was written, by special request, for the Shakespeare Tercentenary number (April 1916) of " Khaki "; a magazine supported by voluntary contributors wholly for the benefit of our fighting men and prisoners of war.

For the verse and prose quotations the old spelling is sometimes used in the MS., at other times the new, and this irregularity has been retained. The proof has been read throughout by Mr. Frank Sidgwick, who has also given much valuable help.

As an editor of Elizabethan and Restoration literature A. H. Bullen may be said to hold a unique place. He worked on broad lines, and his method stands a little apart alike from the meticulous research of later scholars and the rhapsodical eulogies of earlier commentators. The Bullen tradition is so firmly established that some of the papers here

collected together may even seem oddly familiar.
There are, however, many vital points of difference
between Bullen's outlook and that of the critics and
counsellors of to-day, and younger students may be
glad of this opportunity of comparing the two,
instead of being compelled to search the shelves of
reference libraries for the scattered writings of this
true Elizabethan.

Contents

Michael Drayton

Michael Drayton

IT may be expected that in this opening lecture
I should say a few words by way of general
introduction to the series. For the subjects of
the six lectures I have chosen six Elizabethan writers ;
and, to be frank, the names have been taken very
much at random. I do not aim at giving a detailed
account of any particular department of our old
literature ; and far less is it my intention to attempt
to survey the whole field of Elizabethan and Jacobean
poetry. Our old poets were very independent of one
another ; they do not readily fall into classes, and it
seems to me to be better to deal with one author at
a time rather than with whole groups. I have put
Drayton's name first on the list because he is a very
old favourite of mine, and because I think that he
has not received from the moderns the respect that
he deserves. From time out of mind it has been the
custom to couple the name of Daniel with that of
Drayton ; and with true conservative instinct I
have put Daniel's name second on the list. In point
of size Drayton's " Poly-Olbion " is one of the most
considerable achievements of the Elizabethan age. I
can never think of it without calling to mind another
monument of sleepless energy, Chapman's translation
of Homer, and that is how I came to choose Chapman. Dekker I have included because, though his
plays are well known and appreciated, his prose works
—which are full of interest—have been unduly
neglected. As for Nicholas Breton, who is about as
good an example as could be found of an Elizabethan
all-round man of letters, he is hardly known at all.
Dr. Campion, the choicest of the song-writers, was

3

(I venture to think) quite unappreciated even by professed students before I drew attention to his merits in my anthology, " Lyrics from the Song-Books of the Elizabethan Age."

Michael Drayton—one of those names which, as Charles Lamb said, " carry a perfume in the mention "—belonged to Shakespeare's county, Warwickshire, and was born a year before Shakespeare, in 1563, at Hartshill, near Atherstone. Three centuries ago the old Warwickshire poet was a familiar figure in Stratford-on-Avon. For he regularly spent his summers at the Manor House, Clifford Chambers— " the Muse's quiet port," he calls it—with his friends Sir Henry and Lady Rainsford, and we may be sure that in those summer visits to Clifford Chambers (the village lies but a mile or more from Stratford) he saw much of Shakespeare. In 1664, John Ward, Rector, noted among his Memoranda a local tradition that Drayton and Ben Jonson were guests at a banquet at New Place shortly before Shakespeare's death ; and we know that Shakespeare's son-in-law, that famous physician, Dr. John Hall, numbered Drayton among his patients, for has he not left it on record that on one occasion he cured " Mr. Drayton, an excellent poet, of a Tertian ague, by syrop of violets"; fit prescription for a poet ! If we may credit Aubrey, Drayton was the son of a butcher. But the Hartswell Draytons were very possibly a branch of a well-established Leicestershire family, the Draytons of Fenny Drayton, for (in the "Owl," 1603) Drayton speaks of himself as " Nobly bred and well-allied." In a delightful verse-epistle to his friend Henry Reynolds, he tells us something about his early days —how it had been his boyish ambition to become a poet, and how his kindly tutor, so far from checking him, encouraged him in his design, and read him "honest Mantuan" and Virgil's Eclogues when he was

4

Michael Drayton

" . . . a proper goodly page,
Much like a Pigmy, scarse ten years of age."

And the Muses heard his prayer ; they tipped his
tongue with eloquence, filled his heart with fire,
and though fame is capricious and fashions change
he is a true poet, and his name will be held in
honour so long as English literature is studied by
serious students.

To serve as pages in gentlemen's households was
common in those days for boys even of good family ;
and the young Michael Drayton was fortunate in
securing an excellent home and training under the
roof of Sir Henry Goodere at Polesworth Hall, near
Atherstone. Fortunate, yes, and grateful too ; for
he never forgot how much he owed to the master
whose memory he fondly cherished in after years—
"that learn'd and accomplished gentleman, Sir
Henry Goodere, not long since deceased, whose I
was whilst he was, whose patience pleased to bear
with the imperfections of my heedless and unstayed
youth. That excellent and matchless gentleman
was the first cherisher of my muse " ; and in another
place he speaks of " the happy and generous family
of the Gooderes, to which I confess myself beholding
to for the best part of my education." Some critics
have said that Drayton, in early manhood, served
as a soldier ; as to this, " believe as ye list." It is
quite possible that, at his patron's expense, he studied
at one of the Universities: many youths in Elizabethan times were loosely attached to Oxford or
Cambridge without going through a strict curri-
culum or taking a degree, and his friend, Sir Aston
Cokain, claimed him for Oxford. Though he had
not the learning of Ben Jonson, Milton or Gray,
Drayton was a man of wide reading, well versed in
ancient literature, a disciple particularly of the

5

delightful poet Ovid (whom to-day we underrate, but who strongly influenced some of our best English writers) ; a generous critic of our own poets from Chaucer down to his own time ; a close student of French and Italian ; no detractor of modern worth, yet possessed with passionate antiquarian enthusiasm for the greatness of the past.

Seeing how eager he was in boyhood to be numbered among the poets it is curious that he published nothing before 1591, when he was a man of eight-and-twenty. This first book, "The Harmony of the Church," consists of metrical renderings of passages of Scripture ; it has no interest or value, and is merely noteworthy from the fact that it gave offence to the ecclesiastical authorities and was suppressed —nobody knows why—at the instance of the Archbishop of Canterbury, who, notwithstanding, gave orders that forty copies should be preserved at Lambeth Palace.

Perhaps he set but little store by this first volume of verse, for far from being discouraged, he published in 1593 "Idea, the Shepherd's Garland," a collection of eclogues modelled after Spenser's " Shepherd's Calendar." In spite of the "sugared sweetness" of the verse, the reader's ear is again and again vexed by awkward constructions; there are violent inversions in the grammatical order of words ; the subject of a sentence is often left standing without the support of a verb, while with the most arbitrary freedom, participles are used as principal verbs. Yet, undeniably, much of the lyrical part is excellent; and the poems were revised and improved in later editions.

Then come two historical pieces, " The Legend of Gaveston " (1593-4) and the "Legend of Matilda" (1594), written in the somewhat heavy and pedestrian style that the " Mirror for Magistrates," at an earlier date, had brought into vogue. In 1596 both pieces underwent revision, and were re-issued with the addition of " The Tragicall Legend of Robert, Duke of Normandie," a poem that holds some passages of strength and beauty.

The year 1594 brought forth a full harvest, for in addition to " Gaveston " and " Matilda " there was a quaintly pretty poem in rhymed heroics, " Endimion and Phœbe," and the collection of Sonnets " Idea's Mirror," which (like most of Drayton's works) was revised and amplified in later editions. Drayton's Sonnets are, it must be admitted, of varying quality, but some of them are singularly good. The best indeed is so good that Professor Saintsbury—without a shadow of justification—assigns it to Shakespeare. It first appeared in the collection of 1619, and is evidently not early work. Dante Rossetti was, I think, the first to note its marvellous beauty, and well known though this sonnet now is, I will venture to recall it to you :

" Since ther's no helpe come let us kiss and part :
  Nay, I have done ; You get no more of Me ;
  And I am glad, yea glad with all my heart
  That thus so cleanly I my selfe can free.
  Shake hands for ever ; Cancell all our Vowes ;
  And when we meet at any time againe,
  Be it not seen in either of our Browes
  That we one jot of former Love reteyne.
  Now at the last gaspe of Love's latest Breath
  When his Pulse fayling, Passion speechlesse lies,
  When Faith is kneeling by his bed of Death
  And Innocence is closing up his Eyes ;
      Now, if thou would'st, when all have given him
        over,
      From Death to Life thou might'st him yet
        recover."

The lady whom Drayton celebrated as " Idea "

(the Platonic ʼΙδεα, the perfect archetype, ideal perfection) was Ann Goodere, the younger daughter of his patron, Sir Henry Goodere. About the year 1596 she became the wife of Henry (afterwards Sir Henry) Rainsford of Clifford Chambers, Gloucestershire, but Drayton continued to sing her praises in a strain of chivalrous gallantry and devotion long after fervent love had been changed by time into faithful affectionate friendship : it has been said that it was for love of her he never married. Shakespeare's Sonnets were not published until 1609, but we know that some of them were circulated in MS. at a much earlier date ; and there can, to my mind, be no doubt but that Drayton had seen some of these MS. copies. There are occasional resemblances between Shakespeare's Sonnets and Drayton's that are too close to be accidental. Sir Sidney Lee and others think that Shakespeare borrowed from Drayton, but it seems to me that Drayton was the borrower. Dean Beeching and Drayton's biographer, Professor Oliver Elton, have discussed this point, and both agree with me in thinking that the indebtedness is on Drayton's side, not on Shakespeare's. It was customary for Elizabethan sonneteers to imitate French and Italian models, and Sir Sidney Lee has shown that Drayton, like his peers, made free use of French originals. There was no harm in it ; French poets borrowed from Italian without shame, and Italian from the Greek anthology.

In 1595 Sir Henry Goodere died, but before his death he had commended Drayton to the protection of the bountiful Countess of Bedford, who staunchly befriended the poets of her time (Ben Jonson among them). To her Drayton dedicated in 1594 his "Endimion and Phœbe" (a pleasing and graceful poem that he never reprinted), and in 1596 appeared with the dedication to the same patroness, his "Mortimeriados," which in later editions he rechristened "The Barons' Wars." As originally printed it was in seven-line stanzas; but he revised the poem throughout, substituting the *ottava rima*, and in an "Address to the Reader" prefixed to the second edition he gives his reasons for the change. "The cause of this my second greater labour was the insufficient handling of the first, which, though it was more than boldnesse to venture on so noble an argument without leisure and studie competant, eyther of which travaile hardly affords; yet the importunitie of friends made mee contrary to mine owne judgement take, undertake and publish it so as the world hath seene; but heerin I intend not to be too exact, as if either it needed to much excuse (knowing well that even as it was, it ought to have passed for better than some would suffer, who can hardly thinke any thing hath favour but their own, though never so unsavorie) as if I shoulde seeme now to have excelled my selfe, and failing in my hopes to be kept without excuse." The *ottava rima* he declares to be "of all other the most complete and best proportioned. Briefly this sort of stanza hath in it maiestie, perfection and soliditie, resembling the piller which in Architecture is called Tuscan whose shaft is of six diameters & bases of two." The epic took final shape in the 1619 folio, but it cannot be said that the work is a success; it reads better in extracts than as a whole, and is in truth a desert, but a desert well dotted over with green oases. There is a lack of life and movement that makes itself felt, in spite of the excellence of the writing in those glowing coloured stanzas describing the high revels held at Nottingham by Mortimer and Queen Isabella (unhappily too long to quote), and the fine and impressive account of

Edward the Second's last days at Berkeley Castle,
with the dreadful omens and dreams that preluded
his tragic end.

"The ominous Raven often he doth heare,
  Whose croking him of following Horror tells,
Begetting strange imaginarie Feare,
  With heavie Ecchoes like to passing Bells ;
The howling Dogge a doleful Part doth beare
  As though they chym'd his last sad burying Knells ;
    Under his Eave the buzzing Screech-Owle sings,
    Beating the Windowes with her fatall Wings.

"By Night affrighted in his fearefull Dreames
  Of raging Fiends and Goblins that he meets,
Of falling downe from steepe Rocks into Streames,
  Of Deaths, of Buryals and of Wynding Sheets,
Of Wand'ring Helpelesse in farre forraine Realmes,
  Of strong Temptations by seducing Sprights ;
    Wherewith awak'd and calling out for aid
    His hollow Voyce doth make himselfe afraid."

Far more interesting than "The Barons' Wars"
was "England's Heroicall Epistles," first published
in 1597 ; afterwards revised from time to time and
enlarged, it enjoyed great popularity right through
the seventeenth century and on into the eighteenth.
Some of the late editions are on very poor paper,
and were doubtless sold as chapbooks, with "Guy,
Earl of Warwick," "The Seven Champions of
Christendom," and the like.

It is a little discreditable to English scholarship
that no edition of these heroical epistles is generally
accessible to-day. But Drayton himself was largely
to blame, for, like my friend William Butler Yeats,
the Irish poet, he was for ever revising his work,
excising here and adding there, until the stoutest
editor's heart might quail before the task of

producing a satisfactory text. At my suggestion, the Spenser Society of Manchester* many years ago began to reprint Drayton : I warned them that it would be a difficult enterprise, but they went into it courageously, and alas, after having made some progress, were brought to a standstill from the apathy of subscribers. We have since been promised from other hands a definitive edition of Drayton, but—unless some wealthy patron of letters comes to the rescue—years and years may pass before the promise is redeemed.

The "Heroicall Epistles" had for their model Ovid's "Heroides," but Drayton gives us imaginary love letters of actual historical personages (famous in English history), while Ovid's heroes and heroines are drawn from legendary history. The metre employed was the heroic couplet, which is handled with ease and fluency. Drayton's besetting sin was his carelessness in grammatical construction ; to get his rhymes he would not hesitate to make violent and grotesque transpositions of words. But in these "Epistles" the diction is throughout smooth and polished. You can take them up at any point and read on without any sense of fatigue (which could not be said of "The Barons' Wars"), for they are always entertaining, full of life and colour, while in occasional touches of tenderness and pathos the Elizabethan poet proves himself a not unworthy pupil of the skilful Roman artist. Though modern critics have been chary of their praise, certain passages of considerable length are faultless in

* In his Introduction to "Michael Drayton" (printed for the Spenser Society), Professor Oliver Elton says : " Mr. A. H. Bullen has also kindly given me some information privately. No such expert in Elizabethan lore, I have only undertaken this work because Mr. Bullen's other engagements have prevented him from giving his leisure to this one."

execution, and I will now give you an example from the epistle of the Lady Geraldine to her lover, Henry, Earl of Surrey, in Italy.

" With ev'ry little perling breath that blows
How are my thoughts confus'd with joys and woes
As through a gate so through my longing ears
Pass to my heart whole multitudes of fears.
O in a map that I might see thee show
The place where now in danger thou do'st go !
Whilst we discourse, to travel with our eye
Romania, Tuscan and fair Lombardy,
Or with thy pen exactly to set down
The model of that temple or that town ;
And to relate at large where thou hast been
As there and there, and what thou there has seen,
Expressing in a figure by thy hand
How Naples lies, how Florence fair doth stand ;
Or as the Grecians finger dip'd in wine
Drawing a river in a little line,
And with a drop a gulf to figure out
To model Venice moated round about, . . .
· · · · · · ·
Till thou return, the Court I will exchange
For some poor cottage or some country grange,
Where to our distaves as we sit and spin
My maid and I will tell what things have bin ;
Our lutes unstrung shall hang upon the wall,
Our lessons serve to wrap our tow withal ;
And pass the night whiles winter tales we tell
Of many things that long ago befell ;
Or tune such homely carols as were sung
In country sport when we ourselves were young."

About the time when the " Epistles " appeared, Drayton was writing for the stage, usually collaborating with other playwrights. All the plays with the exception of " Sir John Oldcastle " (a play attributed to Shakespeare by a fraudulent publisher) have perished, and I confess I do not think our loss has been very great. There is a tradition that Drayton had a hand in the " Merry Devil of Edmonton " (the tradition is strongly supported by internal evidence), and we know that on the 20th of January, 1598-9, Henslowe advanced him the sum of two pounds on a play to be called " William Longsword." But his heart was not in the work, and he merely took to playwriting as a temporary means of earning his livelihood, and was glad enough to give it up for more congenial writing when the bounty of many patrons and patronesses relieved him from financial anxieties.

Among the friends most helpful to him was one Walter Aston of Tixall, Staffordshire, who, when he was made Knight of the Bath by James the First, appointed Drayton one of his esquires. At James's accession, Drayton had made an attempt to secure some preferment at Court and had written a gratulatory poem to the new king. But his bid for fortune met with failure ; his compliments were treated with contempt and when, the next year, he again tried to gain the king's favour his addresses were again rejected. It is pleasant to know that though the king would do nothing for him, James's son, the chivalrous, high-minded Henry, Prince of Wales, gave Drayton a small pension.

After the publication of the " Owl " Drayton tried a Biblical subject, " Moyses in a Map of his Miracles " (1604), a dull piece of work without any of the quaint touches that redeem his " Noah's Flood " (1630) from unqualified damnation. In 1605 or 1606 (the volume is undated) appeared his " Poems, Lyrick and Pasterall," which contains his fine Odes, among them the first draft of his matchless " Ballad of Agincourt."

" Fair stood the wind for France
  When we our sails advance
  Nor now to prove our chance
    Longer will tarry ;
  But putting to the main
  At Caux, the mouth of Seine,
  With all his martial train
    Landed King Harry.

. . . . . .

" Poitiers and Cressy tell,
  When most their pride did swell,
  Under our swords they fell :
    No less our skill is
  Than when our grandsire great,
  Claiming the regal seat,
  By many a warlike feat,
    Lopp'd the French lilies.

. . . . . .

" On happy Crispin's Day
  Fought was this noble fray
  Which Fame did not delay
    To England to carry.
  O when shall English men
  With such acts fill a pen
  Or England breed again
    Such a King Harry ? "

Next to the " Ballad of Agincourt " we must
place the stirring " Ode to the Virginian Voyage,"
which breathes the finest spirit of patriotism. Very
pleasant, too, are some of the lighter pieces, such
as the " Ode to Cupid," and in the edition of 1619
we find the charming canzonet " To his Coy Love,"
and the good-natured arch verses " To his Rival,"
concluding with the warning—

" What now is thine
    Was only mine,
And first to me was given ;
    Thou laugh'st at me,
    I laugh at thee,
And thus we two are even.

" But I'll not mourn
    But stay my turn ;
The wind may come about, sir,
    And once again
    May bring me in
And help to bear you out, sir."

It is Francis Meres who tells us that Drayton was already engaged upon that vast undertaking which occupied him many years, the "Poly-Olbion," though the first instalment, eighteen books or "Songs," did not appear until 1613, and to these the learned Selden had supplied annotations ; the remaining twelve were all ready for publication by 1619, but were not issued until 1622. Drayton himself, in a characteristic letter to William Drummond of Hawthornden, dated 14th April 1619 explains the cause of delay. " I thank you, my dear, sweet Drummond for your good opinion of *Poly-olbion.* I have done twelve books more ; that is from the 18th Book (which was Kent, if you note it), all the East parts and North to the River Tweed ; but it lieth by me, for the booksellers and I are in terms. They are a company of base knaves whom I both scorn and kick at."

But though scholars and students had delighted in Drayton's *magnum opus*, what honest-thinking man to-day can blame the booksellers of Drayton's day for hesitating before launching the Second Part of " Poly-Olbion," seeing the sales of the First Part had been so discouraging ? It was a mighty task, as the title-page sets out with ceremonious fulness the contents of the stately volume :—

> " POLY-OLBION. / or / *A Chorographicall* Description of *Tracts, Riuers* / *Mountaines, Forests,* and other Parts of this renouned *Isle* / of *Great Britaine,* / With intermixture of the most Remarquable *Stories, Antiquities, Wonders* / *Rarityes, Pleasures and Commodities* of / the same : / *Digested in a Poem* / By / Michael Drayton, / *Esq.*"

Drayton was convinced that this island of ours, this England, was the greatest and most flourishing country in the world, and he filled thirty songs with the tale of its excellencies, eager to save from oblivion every record of its glorious past :—

> So, when injurious Time such monuments doth lose,
> (As, what so great a work by Time that is not
>   wrackt ?),
> We utterly forego that memorable act ;
> But, when we lay it up within the minds of men,
> They leave it their next age, that leaves it hers again.

It must be allowed that generally Drayton had drawn his knowledge of our antiquities from books, and not—like his predecessors Leland and Camden —from first-hand observation ; a modern reader will like best the Thirteenth Song, in which he sings the praises of his native Warwickshire " which so brave spirit hast bred " ; enumerates the birds with loving care, and gives a fine and spirited description of stag hunting. But many people to-day (including some critics) simply cannot read the " Poly-Olbion " ; they find the long rolling alexandrines monotonous, the metre untractable, alien as the hexameter to the genius of the English language.

There is some truth in the charge, but it would be difficult to find a metre possessing at once the variety of blank verse and the travelling speed of the rhymed alexandrine. Again, many people say that the subject matter bores them. It is not a poem from which it is easy to make extracts, though it is a very pleasant book to dip into. When you feel you have had enough of the poetry (and it abounds in passages of rare beauty) you can turn to the notes, at the end of the Songs, which were specially written for Drayton by that profound antiquary (whose "Table-Talk" shows him to be one of the wisest and wittiest of men) John Selden. Finally the "Poly-Olbion" was one of the favourite books of Charles Lamb, and if that be not cogent testimony in its favour, I know not what is. Many years ago, when writing of the "Poly-Olbion," I said that "a saunter down a Surrey lane, when the nuts are ripening, is the one thing pleasanter than a ramble through the 'Poly-Olbion.'" Time adjusts most of our early enthusiasms; still I hold this opinion but little changed.

I could talk for long about "Poly-Olbion," but must hurry on. In 1627 Drayton returned to the subject of Agincourt, this time in a narrative poem which is by no means without interest, but not for a moment comparable with the Ode. In the same volume is an historical poem, "The Miseries of Queen Margarite," which need not detain us; and that sprightly masterpiece of ingenious fancy, the fairy poem "Nimphidia." Transported to Oberon's fairy-court, we instantly forget Queen Margarite and her miseries, for the fairies are in a state of high excitement, and even Herrick's touch was not so dainty as was Drayton's in recounting the doings of the elves. First we have a description of the Fairy Palace.

" This palace standeth in the air,
    By necromancy placed there,
    That it no tempest needs to fear,
        Which way soe'er it blow it ;
    And somewhat southward toward the noon,
    Whence lies a way up to the moon,
    And thence the Fairy can as soon
        Pass to the earth below it."

King Oberon is jealous of the attention paid to the Queen by the fairy knight Pigwiggen. The Queen agrees to meet Pigwiggen by midnight in a cowslip flower, and orders her

" . . . chariot of a snail's fine shell,
        Which for the colours did excel,
        The fair Queen Mab becoming well,
            So lively was the limning ; "

Missing his Queen, Oberon is furious and vows vengeance against Pigwiggen ; in his frenzy he first belabours a wasp, then falls foul of a glow-worm, anon, drives into a hive of bees ; next bestriding an ant makes an assault on a molehill and later tumbles into a lake whence he escapes in an oaken cup. He sends Puck to bring back the queen alive or dead, but meanwhile, he prepares for combat with Pigwiggen, who

" . . . quickly arms him for the field,
        A little cockle-shell his shield,
        Which he could very bravely wield,
            Yet could it not be pierced :
        His spear a bent both stiff and strong,
        And well-near of two inches long :
        The pile was of a horse-fly's tongue,
            Whose sharpness naught reversed.

The fight between Oberon and Pigwiggen is described

with great gusto. Finally Proserpina parts the combatants, gives them a draught of lethe-water to refresh them, and straightway they forget their quarrel, repair to the Fairy Court and fall a-feasting. In reading the " Nimphidia " one is transported to the golden time of childhood, when the air was alive with mystery, when the shadows on the window-blind or the embers in the grate held an Iliad of imaginary joys and sorrows. Few pleasures are better than that of looking back into the delightful world where once we wandered at will; and such a pleasure Michael Drayton has given us in this airy masterpiece of whimsical grace.

Among the most attractive of Drayton's writings are the verse-epistles to various friends, and the most interesting was that addressed to Henry Reynolds (it is in the 1627 volume); Drayton reminds his friend what pleasant hours they had spent together discussing poetry, old and new, and proceeds to pass the English poets in review from Chaucer onwards. Some of his judgments could not be bettered. Mr. Swinburne wrote much in verse and prose in praise of Christopher Marlowe, but Drayton's brief tribute is more effective than Swinburne's lengthy eulogies :—

> " . . . Marlowe, bathed in the Thespian springs,
> Had in him those brave translunary things
> That the first Poets had ; his raptures were
> All air and fire, which made his verses clear ;
> For that fine madness still he did retain
> Which rightly should possess a Poet's brain."

His description of Thomas Nashe, the brilliant satirist, is most apt and happy.

> " . . . though he a Proser were,
> A branch of laurel yet deserves to bear ; "

19

and the contributors to Tottell's Miscellany (the Earl of Surrey, Wyatt, and the others) are well touched off in the phrase, "many dainty passages of wit." After his enthusiastic praise of Marlowe, his lines on Shakespeare strike cold on the ear.

> ". . . . . . be it said of thee
> Shakespeare, thou hadst as smooth a Comick vein
> Fitting the sock, and in thy natural brain,
> As strong conception and as clear a rage
> As any one that traffick'd with the stage."

But Drayton held the ordinary opinion of his time about the inferiority of dramatic writing to other forms of poetry, and, in his praise of Marlowe, was probably thinking more of "Hero and Leander" than of the plays.

Later, in 1630, Drayton again turned to satire with a dull, heavy, ponderous piece of work, "The Moon-calf." It was inevitable that he should fail as a satirical writer, for your genuine satirist takes a delight in exposing the sins and follies of men ; he has generally had more than the mere onlooker's knowledge of the vices he scourges, and so his pen strikes deeper. Of all the sturdy writers gathered round Shakespeare's throne, the most uncleanly is, without doubt, Marston ; yet there was no bitterer assailant of the profligacy of the times than he. Drayton was cast in a different mould. Essentially an unworldly man, he built up round him high walls of romance, and kept his eyes shut to the meanness and villainy practised in the actual world. Not knowing the vulnerable points in his adversaries' armour, his arrows for the most part fly wide of the mark, though occasionally he hits it :—

> " The gripple merchant born to be the curse
> Of this brave isle."

Several of his contemporaries testify to Drayton's honourable and lovable character; he lived a retired life, paid his debts, and was not in perpetual fear of the sheriff's officer, as was poor Dekker, who spent half his life in prison. Francis Meres, writing in 1598, says: " As Aulus Persius Flaccus is reputed among all writers to be of an honest disposition and upright conversation, so Michael Drayton, *quem toties honoris causa nomino*, among scholars, soldiers, poets and all sorts of people, is held for a man of virtuous and self-governed carriage, which is almost miraculous among good wits of this declining and corrupt time "; and the unnamed author of " The Return from Parnassus " tells us " He wants one true note of a poet of our times, and that is this; he cannot swagger it well at a Tavern, or domineer at a hot-house."

The sunny " Muses Elizium " (1630) was the last of Drayton's many volumes. In it he went back to the fairies, and (in the eighth " Nimphall ") gives a delightfully fantastic description of the marriage of a nymph to a fay, that as a play of light fancy is well worthy to stand alongside of the " Nimphidia."

But though the " Muses Elizium " shows no trace of failing power, Drayton was growing old, and the verse-letters, written three years earlier to William Browne of Tavistock (author of " Britannia's Pastorals ") and George Sandys (translator of Ovid's " Metamorphoses "), show that he felt the weight of his years upon him, and the sense of a vague restlessness at the shadow of coming changes: he was looking back along the road he had trodden, and was weighing himself and his work as a man must do when the end is near. Though he had written to William Drummond, " I am more than a fortnight's friend. Where I love, I love for years as I hope you shall find," yet this same " perfect faithful friend" was, in truth, a somewhat lonely man, giving out more affection than he received; and more especially perhaps in his later days, being but little understood even by those who knew him best. He had grown out of touch with his times, if indeed he had ever been at close grips with them. That he " could not swagger it well at a Tavern " meant more than the mere words convey; he lacked the gay spirit of easy comradeship that made the life of cities an absolute necessity for so many Elizabethans, and his " upright conversation " may well not have fitted in with the broad jests and easy jollity of the Mermaid Tavern. Thwarted in love; disappointed at the chilly reception given to his " Poly-Olbion "; contemptuous of the triumph of the sock and buskin which he interpreted as a veritable slight to poetry; unable to understand why men should ever tire of those rolling alexandrines that he loved, the old poet knew it was time for him to leave a world where he was no longer wanted and with whose giant strides he could not hope to keep apace. He died the year after the publication of the " Muses Elizium "; not at Clifford Chambers, "the Muses' quiet port," but in his room with its bay window adjoining St. Dunstan's Church in Fleet Street, and was buried in Westminster Abbey, though nobody knows the exact spot where he lies; pious friends raised a monument to him in Poets' Corner, and tradition says that the inscription was written by Ben Jonson.

In the middle of the eighteenth century a folio of his collected works was published, but he was not to the taste of that " polished and polite " century. In 1742 Pope, writing to Warburton, speaks scornfully of " a very mediocre poet, one Drayton "; and in 1781 Horace Walpole, when he was offered by William Mason a portrait of Drayton for five guineas replied, " I do not think all Drayton ever wrote worth five guineas." Nor is he to the taste of to-day, for he is not widely read and is known to most people only by his " Ballad of Agincourt " and his incomparable love sonnet. The reason may be that the world grows older and life more sombre ; the gospel of Science is spreading, the revels of Oberon have long been broken up, and not the Sicily of Theocritus is more remote from us than the London of Shakespeare.

Yet no poet is more thoroughly English than the writer of the " Poly-Olbion," and in an age remarkable for powerful intellects he held a distinguished place : like some skilled herbalist he cultivated many kinds of poetry, and much of his work is of a rare excellence. He still has some faithful followers who hold, and will ever hold his memory dear ; who will gladly go with him through the gates of Arcady into that old pastoral world where the lark's carol made chorus to fairy music ; and who will still believe (in spite of carping critics) that one of the choicest spirits of the Elizabethan Age was Shakespeare's friend, Michael Drayton.

Samuel Daniel

Samuel Daniel

BEN JONSON told Drummond of Hawthornden that Samuel Daniel was a " good honest man but no poet," and Drayton said of him (in his epistle to Henry Reynolds) :—

" His rhymes were smooth, his metres well did close,
But yet his manner better fitted prose."

Against these severe sayings may be set Coleridge's advice, "Read Daniel—the admirable Daniel " ; and I think that those who follow Coleridge's counsel will employ their time not unprofitably.

Daniel had little of that turbulent, passionate spirit which inspired so many of the Elizabethans. He was of an easy, gentle disposition, naturally fitted to lead a life of lettered leisure ; and he was fortunate in securing through the aid of powerful friends an exemption from the heavy troubles which beset those who had to live and earn their bread by their pen. Somersetshire was his county, and he was born near Taunton in 1562-3. His father, John Daniel, is described by Fuller and others as a music-master. There was a musician and composer John Daniel who published a book of airs in 1606 ; but he was the poet's brother. Whether the father was also a musician has not yet been ascertained, and the point is not of much consequence. In 1579 Samuel became a commoner of Magdalen Hall ; he stayed at Oxford for three years and left without a degree. Anthony Wood explains the absence of the degree by saying in his quaint fashion that Daniel's " geny " was " more prone to easier and smoother studies than in pecking and hewing at logic." There

27

is reason for supposing that after he left Oxford he was received into the family of the Earl of Pembroke at Wilton. The Countess of Pembroke, sister of Sir Philip Sidney and mother of that William Herbert, third Earl of Pembroke, who may be pretty safely identified with the " W. H." of the dedication to Shakespeare's Sonnets, was Daniel's lifelong friend and patroness. In the dedication of his " Defence of Rhyme " (1602) to William Herbert, Daniel speaks with gratitude of the encouragement he had received from the countess in his pursuit of poetry : " Having been first encouraged "—these are his own words—" and framed thereunto by your most worthy and honourable mother, and received the first notion for the formal ordering of these compositions at Wilton, which I must ever acknowledge to have been my best school, and thereof always am to hold a feeling and a grateful memory." In declaring that Wilton was his best school Daniel seems to imply that he owed more to the influence of the cultured society of the countess and her friends than to his regular academic training. It is not known whether he was personally acquainted with Sir Philip Sidney ; but Sidney was a frequent visitor at Wilton, and it is pleasant to think that a friendship may have existed between the two poets.

The first work published by Daniel was a translation of a " worthy tract " of Paulus Jovius on emblems and devices ; it appeared in 1585. Six years afterwards, in 1591, a London publisher, Thomas Newman, brought out a surreptitious edition of Sir Philip Sidney's " Astrophel and Stella " sonnets, with an epistle to the reader by the redoubtable Tom Nashe, and " Sundry other rare sonnets by divers noblemen and gentlemen." Among these " sundry other rare sonnets " were twenty-seven of Daniel's sonnets to Delia. Making this unauthorised publication his excuse, Daniel issued in 1592 the series of the Delia sonnets, fifty in number, to which he appended "The Complaint of Rosamond." Prefixed is a prose epistle to the Countess of Pembroke which begins thus : " Right Honourable, although I rather desired to keep in the private passions of my youth from the multitude as things uttered to myself and consecrated to silence : yet seeing I was betrayed by the indiscretion of a greedy printer, and had some of my secrets bewrayed to the world uncorrected, doubting the like of the rest I am forced to publish that which I never meant." This tone of apology runs through much of Elizabethan literature. Poets constantly asserted that they wrote merely to please themselves and to be read by their select friends. Occasionally these protestations were no doubt genuine. For instance, when Sir Philip Sidney on his death-bed directed that his unpublished romance " Arcadia " should be destroyed, his sincerity could not for a moment be questioned. But I do hold distinctly that in most cases this seeming reluctance to appear in print was mere affectation. Michael Drayton has some scornful remarks on this point in his epistle to Henry Reynolds :—

" To such whose poems, be they ne'er so rare,
    In private chambers that encloistered are,
    And by transcription daintily must go
    As though the world unworthy were to know
    Their rich composures, let those men that keep
    These wondrous relics in their judgment deep
    And cry them up so, let such pieces be
    Spoke of by those that shall come after me :
    I hope not for them."

People are apt, too apt indeed, to think that age improves poetry as surely as it improves port ; but the vintage of the Muses does not depend upon careful cellarage. The view that I have formed after long inquiry, extending over years, is that the best Elizabethan poetry—I do not speak of the plays, for there the case may be different—almost invariably found its way into print, and I doubt whether ever so careful a search by students of the future among records of the past will bring to light many more treasures of golden verse than the great Elizabethan age has already given us. In public and private libraries are preserved numerous collections of MS. poetry of the Elizabethan and Jacobean age. I have personally examined scores, or I may say without exaggeration hundreds of such MSS.; but I have constantly found that with very few exceptions everything of worth in these collections is accessible in printed form. Hence I cannot believe that those old poets who affected such anxiety to shun publicity were as modest as they pretended to be; they knew what good work they were doing and were doubtless mighty proud of themselves. Daniel, it is true, had reason to complain of the imperfect and mutilated form in which his sonnets were given to the public by the greedy publisher, but I suspect that he was well pleased at having so good an excuse for courting popular applause. His sonnets were very favourably received; a second edition appeared in the same year, a third in 1594, and they were frequently reprinted in his later collections, with a few additions.

The form of sonnet that Daniel adopted was that of four separate quatrains followed by a couplet; and it has been thought that his example may have helped to fix the form of the Shakespearean sonnets. Daniel's sonnets are careful, polished compositions, the work of one who was above everything a *verborum artifex*—a master of language, and William Browne, in "Britannia's Pastorals," invented for him a most felicitous epithet—"well-languaged Daniel." We shall not discover in his sonnets the rich imagery, the gorgeous colouring that we have in Spenser's, nor the fervour and exaltation of spirit that ennobled the sonnets of Sidney; but they are infinitely better than the tawdry, frigid conceits of that much-belauded sonnetteer, Thomas Watson. They can all be read with pleasure, but they leave no abiding trace in the memory (that truest test of true poetry), unless we make exception for the one beginning "Care-charmer Sleep, son of the sable night," which has found its way into many anthologies. The opening sonnet, "Unto the boundless ocean of thy beauty," is derided in "Everyman in his Humour"; but Ben Jonson had a grudge against Daniel and was often girding at him. In spite of Jonson's sneer I think that it is not a bad sonnet, and that it forms an appropriate introduction to the others. But perhaps the following is a fairer specimen to quote :—

" Let others sing of knights and Palladines
    In aged accents and untimely words ;
Paint shadows in imaginary lines,
    Which well the reach of their high wits records ;
But I must sing of thee, and those fair eyes
    Authentic shall my verse in time to come,
While yet th' unborn shall say ' Lo, where she lies
    Whose beauty made him speak who else was
        dumb.'
These are the arks, the trophies I erect,
    That fortify thy name against old age :
And these thy sacred virtues must protect
    Against the dark and time's consuming rage.
Though th' error of my youth in them appear,
Suffice they shew I lived and loved thee dear."

From two of the sonnets it appears that Daniel had

been in Italy some time before 1592—possibly he
went in charge of young William Herbert.

Following the sonnets is a pleasing lyric, which
Daniel somewhat arbitrarily calls an " ode," of
which the first stanza was set to music by John
Farmer in 1599. It is very tunable verse :—

" Now each creature joys the other,
　　Passing happy days and hours;
One bird reports unto another
　　In the fall of silver showers ;
Whilst the earth (our common mother)
　　Hath her bosom decked with flowers.

" Whilst the greatest torch of heaven
　　With bright rays warms Flora's lap,
Making nights and days both even,
　　Cheering flowers with fresher sap,
My field, of flowers quite bereaven,
　　Wants refresh of better hap.

" Echo, daughter of the air,
　　Babbling guest of rocks and hills,
Knows the name of my fierce fair
　　And sounds the accents of my ills ;
Each thing pities my despair
　　Whilst that she her lover kills.

" Whilst that she, O cruel maid,
　　Doth me and my true love despise,
My life's flourish is decayed,
　　That depended on her eyes ;
But her will must be obeyed,
　　And well he ends for love who dies."

After this comes a well-written and interesting little
poem headed " A Pastoral." It is in stanzas of

thirteen lines of varied lengths; the metre is effective, and Daniel might have employed it oftener with advantage. Of course, like all the poets of his time, he was well acquainted with Italian literature; and the metrical structure of this poem is closely modelled on the tenth canzone of Petrarch.

" O happy golden age,
  Not for that rivers ran
  With streams of milk, and honey dropped from
      trees ;
  Not that the earth did gage
  Unto the husband-man
  Her voluntary fruits, free without fees :
  Not for no cold did freeze,
  Nor any cloud beguile
  Th' eternal flow'ring spring
  Wherein lived everything,
  And whereon th' heavens perpetually did smile ;
  Not for no ship had brought
  From foreign shores or wars or wares ill-sought :
  But only for that name
  That idle name of wind,
  That idol of deceit, that empty sound
  Called Honor, which became
  The tyran of the mind,
  And so torments our nature without ground,
  Was not yet vainly found,
  Nor yet sad griefs imparts
  Amidst the sweet delights
  Of joyful amorous wights,
  Nor were his hard laws known to free-born hearts."

There is no need to dwell on " The Complaint of Rosamond," an easy, ambling poem, well turned, in six-line stanzas. The " Mirror for Magistrates " had set the fashion for this sort of writing, and one of the best specimens that we have is Churchyard's

"Legend of Jane Shore," an excellent companion piece to "The Complaint of Rosamond" and to some of Drayton's legends. The Ghost of Rosamond in Daniel's poem is called from the shadows of black night to repeat the story of her sins and sorrows ; she tells her tale in pure, fluent English with a pathetic tenderness that wins our pity ; but it must be confessed that this sort of poetry, even when ably handled—as by Churchyard, and Daniel, and Drayton—soon becomes wearisome and insipid.

When the sonnets and Rosamond were reprinted in 1594 they were accompanied by "Cleopatra," a tragedy written on the model of Seneca. Another piece of similar character was the tragedy of "Philotas," published in 1605. Seneca was very much praised in Elizabethan times, but luckily he was more praised than imitated. A few stock lines— "*Curae leves loquuntur ingentes stupent*" and the like— were in brisk demand, and occasionally in Webster, more frequently in Marston, we find reminiscences of Seneca ; but Daniel was one of the very few who deliberately, in cold blood, composed plays on the Senecan model. The Countess of Pembroke had published "The Tragedy of Antony" from the French of Garnier. Daniel, dedicating "Cleopatra" to the countess, expressly states that it was written as a companion piece to "Antony." Of dramatic movement there is absolutely nothing, but the play was intended for the study, not for the stage. Long-winded monologues and the moralising of the chorus—this is the fare provided. But the choruses gave Daniel a good opportunity of indulging his sententious vein, and if we suppose that "Cleopatra" was composed rather as a compliment to the Countess of Pembroke than from any liking for the subject, we may yet feel confident that the writing of the choruses sweetened Daniel's labour. "Philotas,"

the second play, is a stronger piece of work than
" Cleopatra," and is not altogether without dramatic interest. The writing of it brought Daniel
into difficulties, for in the person of the aspiring
Philotas, who was put to death by Alexander the
Great on suspicion of treasonable practices, the
Earl of Essex was supposed to be represented ; and
Daniel was summoned before the Lords of the Privy
Council. When he published the play in 1605 he
appended an apology in which he protests against
" the wrong application and misconceiving of this
tragedy of Philotas." He declared that more than
eight years since he had communicated his intention
of writing on the subject of Philotas to his friend
Dr. Latware, " who said that himself had written
the same argument and caused it to be presented
in St. John's College in Oxford : where, as I after
heard, it was worthily and with great applause
performed."

The doctor and others urged Daniel to prosecute
his design. This would be in 1596. Four years
afterwards, living in the country, he wrote the first
three acts, " near half a year," he assures us, before
"the late tragedy of ours"—namely Essex's rebellion,
arraignment and execution. He further states that
he wrote the play with the purpose of having it
represented in Bath " by certain gentlemen's sons
as a private recreation for the Christmas before the
Shrovetide of that unhappy disorder" (that would
be the Christmas of 1600), but being called upon by
the publisher for a new edition of his poems he let
the tragedy slide and composed some new additions
for his poems on " The Civil Wars." Before the
Privy Council he defended himself by declaring that
the MS. of the play had passed through the hands
of the Master of the Revels, and that he had read
portions of it himself to Lord Mountjoy. It appears

that Lord Mountjoy did not relish his name being introduced in connection with the matter, for among the state papers there is a letter written in 1604 by Daniel to Mountjoy, who had meanwhile been created Earl of Devonshire. Daniel begins by expressing regret that he should have given offence to his lordship in connection with the matter of Philotas, and explains, " I said I had read some part of it to your honour, and this I said having none else of power to grace me now in court and hoping that you, out of your knowledge of books or favour of letters and me, might answer that there is nothing in it disagreeing nor anything, as I protest there is not, but out of the universal notions of ambition and envy, the perpetual arguments of books of tragedies. I did not say that you encouraged me unto the presenting of it ; if I should I had been a villain, for that when I showed it to your honour I was not resolved to have had it acted, nor should it have been had not my necessities overmastered me." All this is very bewildering, especially the last sentence. Daniel had never written, so far as is known, for the stage ; and when there were so many practised playwrights about, there was no need to call his pen into play. But it would appear from this letter that " Philotas " had been acted, and that Daniel had derived some pecuniary advantage from the representation—" nor should it have been had not my necessities overmastered me." The play is not very attractive, and I cannot think that— but for the supposed allusions to Essex—it could have gained a hold on any audience. Daniel is careful to state that the first three acts had been written before the Essex troubles ; but it seems to me that the fourth act contains the strongest passages and was most likely to arouse protest. When Philotas defends himself with eloquence before his peers from the charge of treason, the thoughts of the audience would be turned to Essex, the ill-starred, passionate soldier, who had so often fought for England :—

" God forbid that ever soldiers' words
    Should be made liable unto misdeeds ;
    When fainting in their march, tired in the fight,
Sick in their tent, stopping their wounds that bleeds,
Or haught and jolly after conquest got,
    They shall out of their heart use words unkind,
    Their deeds deserve to have them rather thought
The passion of the season than their mind ;
For soldiers' joy or wrath is measureless,
    Wrapt with an instant motion ; and we blame,
    We hate, we praise, we pity in excess
According as our present passions frame.
Sometimes to pass the Ocean we would fain,
    Sometimes to other worlds, and sometimes slack
    And idle, with our conquests, entertain
A sullen humour of returning back :
All which conceits one trumpet's sound doth end,
    And each man running, to his rank, doth lose
    What in our tents disliked us, and we spend
All that conceived wrath upon our foes.
And words, if they proceed of levity,
    Are to be scorned, of madness pitied,
    If out of malice or of injury
To be remissed or unacknowledged,
For of themselves they vanish by disdain."

The watchfulness of the authorities in those days was very keen ; and at a time when public excitement was running high it is not surprising that steps should have been taken to stop the performance of a play that was likely to excite lively sympathy for Elizabeth's fallen favourite. But Essex's rebellion was quickly forgotten, and when the play was

37

printed in 1605 Daniel boldly dedicated it to the young Prince Henry. This dedication is in his best manner. As the prince was only ten years of age at the time he could hardly be expected to appreciate such a piece of work as " Philotas " ; but Daniel was at pains to impress upon him early that it behoves princes to encourage and honour letters :—

" For know, great prince, when you shall come to
    know
  How that it is the fairest ornament
  Of worthy times to have those which may show
  The deeds of power, and lively represent
  The actions of a glorious government ;
  And is no lesser honour to a crown
  T' have writers than have actors of renown."

Daniel looks forward to the day when Prince Henry will " grace this now neglected harmony," but he does not expect himself to be spared to see that happy time. For his own part he lives rather in the past than in the future ; he looks wistfully to the golden age of Elizabeth and mourns for the vanished splendour :—

" Though I, the remnant of another time,
  Am never like to see that happiness,
  Yet, for the zeal that I have born to rhyme
  And to the Muses, wish that good success
  To others' travail, that in better place
  And better comfort they may be incheer'd,
  Who shall deserve and who shall have the grace
  To have a Muse held worthy to be heard.
  And know, sweet Prince, when you shall come to
    know,
  That 'tis not in the power of kings to raise
  A spirit for verse that is not born thereto,
  Nor are they born in every prince's days ;

For late Eliza's reign gave birth to more
Than all the kings of England did before.
And it may be the Genius of that time
Would leave to her the glory in that kind,
And that the utmost powers of English rhyme
Should be within her peaceful reign confined ;
For since that time our songs could never thrive
But lain as if forlorn ; though in the prime
Of this new raising season we did strive
To bring the best we could unto the time.
And I, although among the latter train,
And least of those that sung unto this land,
Have borne my part, though in an humble strain,
And pleased the gentler that did understand,
And never had my harmless pen at all
Distained with any loose immodesty,
Nor ever noted to be touched with gall
To aggravate the worst man's infamy ;
But still have done the fairest offices
To virtue and the time : yet naught prevails,
And all our labours are without success ;
For either favour or our virtue fails.
And therefore since I have outlived the date
Of former grace, acceptance, and delight,
I would my lines late-born beyond the fate
Of her spent line had never come to light.
So had I not been taxed for wishing well,
Nor now mistaken by the censuring stage,
Nor in my fame and reputation fell,
Which I esteem more than what all the age
Or th' earth can give. But years hath done this
    wrong
To make me write too much and live too long."

Noble, memorable verse, which none can read
without feeling that he who wrote it was at once
a true poet and a man of stainless honour.

I thought it well to consider the two plays together, but in thus dealing with " Philotas " I have not kept to chronological order. Daniel's longest, but not, I think, his most interesting poem, is his " Civil Wars between the two Houses of Lancaster and York." The first four books appeared in 1595 ; a fifth followed in 1599. In the 1601 folio edition of his works the five books were redistributed and converted into seven ; an eighth book was added in 1609. The text of the various editions differs considerably, for Daniel, like Drayton, was fond of revising his work. To the edition of 1609 he prefixed a dedicatory prose epistle to his old patroness the Countess Dowager of Pembroke. The " Civil Wars " was one of the poems which Coleridge specially urged people to read ; but it needs much patience and a stout heart to do as Coleridge bids us. When one has praised the purity of the language and admired the metrical skill shown in the handling of the eight-line stanzas, I am not aware that there is much more to be said. Drayton reports that he had heard some " wise men " declare that Daniel was " too much historian in verse." The censure is just, but sounds odd from the lips of Drayton, whose " Barons' Wars " is open to precisely the same criticism. Ben Jonson wittily observed to Drummond that " Daniel wrote ' Civil Wars ' and yet hath not a battle in all his book." We would fain catch some Homeric echoes and hear for once the clash of meeting swords ; but Daniel's narrative flows on and on and on, smooth, clear, with not a wrinkle on the surface, until while we wish it had never been begun, we can see no reason in the world why it should ever end.

If we want to gain a true appreciation of Daniel's power, we must not go to the " Civil Wars " but to " Musophilus, a General Defence of all Learning."

This poem (issued in 1602 or 1603 and fitly dedicated to Fulke Greville, Lord Brooke, a man whose genius bore some affinity to Daniel's) takes the form of a colloquy. Philocosmus tries to draw Musophilus from the " ungainful art " of poetry to more practical pursuits ; and Musophilus in a strain of lofty and impassioned eloquence vindicates his allegiance to the Muses. It would be difficult to name a poem of equal compass—there are something under a thousand lines—which contains so copious a store of weighty reflections dressed in language so decorous. Towards the close, in a passage of startling grandeur, the poet looks forward in imagination like some inspired seer to the time when our English speech will have been carried to shores then unknown :—

" Power above powers, O heavenly Eloquence,
  That with the strong rein of commanding words,
  Dost manage, guide, and master th' eminence
  Of men's affections more than all their swords :
  Shall we not offer to thy excellence
  The richest treasure that our wit affords ?
  That thou canst do much more with one poor pen
  Than all the powers of princes can effect,
  And draw, divert, dispose and fashion men
  Better than force or rigour can direct :
  Should we this ornament of glory then
  As th' unmaterial fruit of shades neglect ?
  Or should we careless come behind the rest
  In power of words that go before in worth,
  Whenas our accents, equal to the best,
  Is able greater wonders to bring forth ;
  When all that ever hotter spirits exprest
  Comes bettered by the patience of the North.
  And who in time knows whither we may vent
  The treasure of our tongue, to what strange shores
  The gain of our best glory shall be sent

T' enrich unknowing Nations with our stores ?
What worlds in the yet unformed Occident
May come refined with th' accents that are ours ?
Or who can tell for what great work in hand
The greatness of our style is now ordained ?
What powers it shall bring in, what spirits com-
    mand,
What thoughts let out, what humours keep re-
    strained ?
What mischiefs it may powerfully withstand,
And what fair end may thereby be attained."

The poem is of such sustained dignity that it is
difficult to know what passages to select. Reflecting
how time turns human monuments to mockery,
Daniel is reminded of Stonehenge, which he must
have often visited when he was staying at Wilton :—

" And whereto serve[s] that wondrous trophy now
    That on the goodly plain near Wilton stands ?
    That huge dumb heap that cannot tell us how,
    Nor what, nor whence it is, nor with what hands,
    Nor for whose glory it was set to show
    How much our pride mocks that of other lands ?
    Whereon whenas the gazing passenger
    Hath greedy looked with admiration
    And fain would know his worth and what he were
    How there erected and how long agone ;
    Enquires and asks his fellow-traveller
    What he hath heard, and his opinion ;
    And he knows nothing. Then he turns again,
    And looks, and sighs, and then admires afresh,
    And in himself with sorrow doth complain
    The misery of dark forgetfulness ;
    Angry with Time that nothing should remain
    Our greatest wonders' wonder to express."

Wordsworth, who was a great admirer of Daniel,

borrowed from " Musophilus " for one of his river
Duddon sonnets the magnificent line—

" Sacred Religion, mother of form and fear."

With " Musophilus " should be read the " Epistles "
which Daniel describes as written " after the
manner of Horace." The finest of them is to the
Countess of Cumberland ; it consists of sixteen
eight-line stanzas, and every stanza is freighted with
a wealth of ethical wisdom—" infinite riches in a
little room." Very beautiful too is that to the
Countess's daughter, Lady Anne Clifford. Daniel
was her tutor from 1600 to 1602 ; and she was
about twelve years old when the poem was written.
Others are to Sir Thomas Egerton (afterwards Lord
Ellesmere) ; to Lord Henry Howard ; to the
Countess of Bedford ; and to Lord Southampton.
The fine elegy on the " Earl of Devonshire," 1606,
should also be read in connection with " Musophilus " and the " Epistles."

It is said that Daniel on the death of Spenser in
1599 was appointed poet-laureate, and though it
cannot be shown that there was any formal appointment, his services appear to have been in demand
from time to time when entertainments at Court
were required. On the accession of James in 1603
Daniel presented him with a " panegyric congratu-
latory " which is marked by a tone of manly in-
dependence. The new queen, Queen Anne, appointed
him one of her grooms of the Privy Chamber, an
office that carried no great responsibility but
provided him with a competence. Some of his
biographers say that he got this preferment through
the influence of John Florio, whom they style his
brother-in-law ; but there is no evidence to prove
that Florio was his brother-in-law, or that Florio had
sufficient influence to procure him the appointment.

In an address to "Her Sacred Majesty" he speaks gratefully of the favour he had received :—

> " I who by that most blessèd hand sustained,
> In quietness do eat the bread of rest ;
> And by that all-reviving power obtained
> That comfort which my Muse and me hath
>   blessed."

In 1604 he held some post, probably of a temporary character, in the office of the Master of the Revels, in connection with the licensing of plays ; and in 1615, at the instance of the queen, he was privileged to train a company of youths at Bristol for the performance of comedies and tragedies, under the name of the "Youths of Her Majesty's Royal Chamber of Bristol." Altogether he seems to have been in fairly comfortable circumstances. Fuller says that he had a house in the suburbs of London where he used to seclude himself for months together when he was at work on his poems : " As the tortoise burieth himself all the winter in the ground, so Mr. Daniel would be hid at his garden house in Old Street near London for some months together, the more retiredly to enjoy the company of the Muses ; and then would appear in public to converse with his friends, whereof Dr. Cowel and Mr. Camden were principal."

It remains to say a few words about Daniel's Masques and entertainments. "The Vision of the Twelve Goddesses," performed at Hampton Court in 1604, gave satisfaction from the costly manner in which it was mounted ; but it is of slender interest. "The Queen's Arcadia," presented before the Queen here in Oxford, at Christ Church, in August, 1605, is a graceful pastoral play ; it is not for a moment to be compared with Fletcher's " Faithful Shepherdess " or Jonson's " Sad Shepherd," but it is distinctly good work. "Tethys Festival," a masque presented at Whitehall in 1610, contains one fine lyric, "Are they shadows which we see?" That was quoted in Charles Lamb's "Specimens of Dramatic Authors." But the best of Daniel's entertainments is "Hymen's Triumph," 1615, written to grace the nuptials of Lord Roxburgh, a delicate little pastoral comedy, interspersed with songs.

Four years after the publication of "Hymen's Triumph"—in 1619—Daniel died at Beckington, in Somersetshire. It is not known at what time he retired into the country; but Fuller says that he devoted his closing days to farming. Years afterwards his pupil, the Lady Anne Clifford of early days, placed a mural monument to his memory at Beckington Church, with this inscription:—

"Here lies, expecting the second coming of our Lord and Saviour Jesus Christ, the dead body of Samuel Daniel, Esq., that excellent poet and historian who was tutor to the Lady Anne Clifford in her youth, she that was sole daughter and heir to George Clifford, Earl of Cumberland; who in gratitude to him erected this monument to his memory a long time after when she was Countess Dowager of Pembroke, Dorset and Montgomery. He died in October, 1619."

I have left myself but scant space to speak of Daniel's prose. His "Defence of Rhyme," published in 1602, was written in answer to Campion's "Observations in the Art of English Poesy." It is an admirable critical treatise, tasteful, judicious, and convincing. His "History of England," from the Roman occupation to the reign of Edward IV, has (I suppose) little, if any, value as history; but it will be read, by the few, for its literary merits. It contains no passages of such impressive eloquence, such towering grandeur, as we find in Sir Walter Raleigh's " History of the World " ; but it is written in clear, undefiled English, and in the seventeenth century was greatly esteemed. Gerard Langbaine in his account of Daniel said that " however his genius was qualified for poetry, I take his history to be the crown of all his works "—a judgment in which he is likely to remain singular.

It is hardly to be expected that Daniel will ever be popular again ; but he will live in the affection of students and men of letters. They will admire his invariable felicity of diction, his polish and refinement ; and they know that—twice at least—in " Musophilus " and the Epistle to the Countess of Cumberland he attained that large utterance that belongs only to the masters of song. Few men have ever cultivated literature with the frank, wholehearted devotion of Samuel Daniel—literature for its own sake, and not for what it may bring of advantage or reward. He was impressed with the dignity of his high calling ; he knew that a perfect poem outlives the downfall of dynasties, and he longed to be numbered with those who have spoken things worthy of Apollo. His " Civil Wars " and his Senecan tragedies may be forgotten, but his eloquent poems in Learning's praise will live as long as Learning is respected.

George Chapman

George Chapman

GEORGE CHAPMAN is a difficult writer, and must be studied carefully if he is studied at all; and we shall need all our patience, for the obscurities that confront us in Chapman's work are formidable. He wrote a vast deal, but some of his writings may be safely neglected. In the present lecture I will try to guide you as best I can through the wilderness.

Chapman was born near Hitchin, about 1559. William Browne, in the second book of "Britannia's Pastorals," styles him "the learned Shepherd of fair Hitchin Hill." Anthony Wood (who wrongly supposed that he came of a Kentish family) is confident that he was educated at Oxford, and it is usually assumed that he spent some time at Oxford and afterwards went to Cambridge. Wood writes: "In 1574 or thereabouts he, being well grounded in school learning, was sent to the university, but whether first to this in Oxon or that of Cambridge is to me unknown; sure I am that he spent some time at Oxon, where he was observed to be most excellent in the Latin and Greek tongues, but not in logic or philosophy, and therefore I presume that that was the reason why he took no degree." Warton, in his "History of English Poetry," says that he passed two years at Trinity College, Oxford. As Warton was himself a Trinity man he may have had access to some special source of information; but his statement has never been corroborated, so far as I know, and there is no mention of Chapman in any of the valuable lists recently published by the Oxford Historical Society.

His first work, a very harsh piece of writing, was
" Skia Nuktos. The Shadow of Night : containing
two poetical hymns," published in 1594. From the
minuteness with which, in the second hymn, he
describes an incident of Sir Francis Vere's campaign
in the Netherlands, it has been suggested that he
served under Vere as a volunteer. Appended to the
hymn are some glosses, which so far from throwing
light on the obscurities, only intensify the darkness.
His next work, " Ovid's Banquet of Sense " and
other poems, 1595, is equally obscure, but contains
good verse if we are willing to dig for it. The
" Banquet " seems to have been held in high esteem,
for no less than twenty-five quotations from it are
given in the well-known anthology, " England's
Parnassus." Perhaps the obscurest of all Chapman's
writings is a " Coronet for his Mistress Philosophy,"
which followed the " Banquet," a series of sonnets ;
beneath the last sonnet is written *Lucidius olim*—a
promise that the poet will be clearer hereafter. The
" Amorous Zodiac," in the same volume, is a
singularly frigid poem in the praise of an imaginary
mistress. In 1596 Chapman prefixed a poem in
blank verse of some two hundred lines entitled
"*De Guiana Carmen Epicum*" to Lawrence Keymes's
relation of the " Second Voyage to Guiana." This
is the first of Chapman's poems that can be read
with any comfort. There is a fine ring in it, and it
glows with patriotic enthusiasm ; but the language
is not so clear and straightforward as might be
wished. In 1598 appeared the first edition of
Marlowe's fragment of " Hero and Leander," and
it was followed in the same year by an edition of the
whole poem as completed by Chapman. To Chapman's continuation is prefixed a dedicatory epistle
(found only in this edition of 1598) to Lady Walsingham, whose favours are gratefully acknowledged. A

passage in the third sestiad would lead us to suppose
that Marlowe had asked Chapman to complete the
poem. The passage runs thus :—

" Then thou, most strangely intellectual fire,
   That, proper to my soul, hath power t' inspire
   Her burning faculties, and with the wings
   Of thy unsphered flame visit'st the springs
   Of spirits immortal ! now (as swift as time
   Doth follow motion) find th' eternal clime
   Of his free soul whose living subjects stood
   Up to the chin in the Pierian flood,
   And drunk to me half this Musæan story,
   Inscribing it to deathless memory :
   Confer with it, and make my pledge as deep
   That neither's draught be consecrate to sleep ;
   Tell it how much his late desires I tender
   (If yet it know not) and to light surrender
   My soul's dark offspring."

This is fine verse, but it is not too intelligible. The
words "late desires" can hardly refer to any
solemn death-bed utterance of Marlowe, for we
know that his end was fearfully sudden. " And
drunk to me half this Musæan story" means that
Marlowe had read his unfinished poem to Chapman ;
and I suppose " his late desires " refers to some
conversation in which Marlowe expressed a wish
that in the event of his death Chapman should edit
and complete the poem, a duty which Chapman
pledged himself to perform. The closing words,
" and to light surrender My soul's dark offspring,"
seem to me intelligible. The " soul's dark offspring "
is Chapman's continuation of the poem, the last
four sestiads as yet undisclosed to public view ; and
" to light surrender " merely means set forth in
print. In Chapman's continuation—notably in the
Tale of Teras in the fifth sestiad—there are some

clusters of musical verse ; but the tedious conceits and ill-timed moralising are obtruded with astonishing perversity.

The precise date when, as an old writer puts it, " learned George Chapman was forced to write for the stage " is unknown. Meres in 1598 mentions him as one of the best writers of tragedy and comedy. The earliest notice of him in Henslowe's Diary is under date 12 February, 1595-6, on which day was brought out " The Blind Beggar of Alexandria," printed in 1598. This is the least valuable of Chapman's plays, a clumsy piece of work with a preposterous plot, but it appears from the Diary to have been very profitable to Henslowe, and to have invariably drawn large audiences. In June, 1598, he was engaged on a play called " The Will of a Woman," and in the following autumn he wrote " The Fount of New Fashions "; both plays are lost.

There is a curious entry in the Diary under date 2 July, 1599, of a final payment to Chapman of thirty shillings (he had been paid previously some sums on account) for " his book called The World runs o' Wheels, and now All Fools but the Fool." The explanation is that a play originally called " The World runs on Wheels " had been rechristened " All Fools but the Fool " ; and this may be identified with that admirable comedy, the best of all Chapman's plays, published in 1605—having meanwhile, probably, undergone revision—under the title of " All Fools." It is both well constructed and well written, one of the most orderly and artistic comedies of the Elizabethan age. Oddly enough, Chapman seems to have attached but little value to it, for in the dedication to Sir Thomas Walsingham (which was almost immediately cancelled and is found in very few copies) he speaks of it as " the least allowed birth of my shaken brain." Yet the dialogue is brisk and bright, the situations diverting, and the plot skilfully conducted—although, perhaps, the conclusion is somewhat huddled. Beautiful poetry abounds,—as in this passage in praise of Love when Valerio is rebuking Rinaldo, who has spoken in dispraise of womankind :—

" I tell thee Love is Nature's second sun,
  Causing a spring of Virtues where he shines ;
  And as without the sun, the world's great eye
  All colours, beauties, both of art and nature,
  Are given in vain to men, so without love
  All beauties bred in women are in vain,
  All virtues born in men lie buried,
  For love informs them as the sun doth colours ;
  And as the sun, reflecting his warm beams
  Against the earth, begets all fruits and flowers,
  So love, fair shining in the inward man,
  Brings forth in him the honourable fruits
  Of valour, wit, virtue, and haughty thoughts,
  Brave resolution, and divine discourse.
  O 'tis the Paradise, the heaven of earth,
  And didst thou know the comfort of two hearts
  In one delicious harmony united,
  As to joy one joy, and think both one thought,
  Live both one life, and therein double life ;
  To see their souls met at an interview
  In their bright eyes, at parley in their lips ;
  Thou wouldst abhor thy tongue for blasphemy."

Chapman's next play, " An Humorous Day's Mirth," written and published in 1599, is vastly inferior in every way to " All Fools," though it is better than the " Blind Beggar."

About this time he seems to have withdrawn himself temporarily from the stage in order to work more closely at his translation of Homer. The first instalment appeared in 1598, " Seven Books of the

Iliads of Homer, Prince of Poets. Translated according to the Greek in judgment of his best commentaries," with a dedication to the Earl of Essex. It comprises books I-II, VII-XI inclusive. Chapman's dedicatory epistles are always worth reading, and this to Essex is of much dignity. In it he speaks of his straitened circumstances and of the neglect shown to learning. The metre adopted was rhymed verse of fourteen syllables, into which he afterwards turned the whole Iliad. Later in 1598 he published " Achilles' Shield," translated from the eighteenth book of the Iliad : and in the dedicatory epistle to Essex he defends Homer most vigorously from the assaults of " soul-blind " Scaliger, for whom he exhibits a most profound contempt. " Achilles' Shield " was turned into ten-syllabled, rhymed lines, the metre afterwards employed in the translation of the Odyssey.

It was not until 1609 that Chapman published his translation of the first twelve books of the Iliad. Prefixed are a fine dedicatory epistle in verse to Prince Henry, a sonnet to Queen Anne, and a Poem to the Reader. At the end of the book are fourteen sonnets to noble patrons. On the 8th of April, 1611, the complete translation was entered on the Stationers' Register, and was probably published in the same year, though the title-page is undated. The translation of books I and II, down to the catalogue of the ships, had been rewritten, and it appears from the Preface to the Reader that the last twelve books were translated in the space of fifteen weeks— no ordinary feat.

It had been whispered in some quarters that Chapman made his translation, not from the original Greek, but from Latin or French versions. He was highly indignant at this insinuation—" the frontless detractions of some stupid ignorants, that no more

knowing me than their own beastly ends, and I ever
(to my knowledge) blest from their sight, whispered behind me vilifyings of my translation[s];
out of the French affirming them, when both in
French and all other languages but his own, our
with-all-skill-enriched poet is so poor and unpleasing
that no man can discern from whence flowed his so
generally given eminence and admiration.   And
therefore (by any reasonable creature's conference
of my slight comment and conversation) it will
easily appear how I shun them and whether the
original be my rule or not ; in which he shall easily
see I understand the understandings of all other
interpreters and commentators in places of his most
depth, importance and rapture. In whose exposition
and illustration, if I abhor from the sense that others
wrest and rack out of him, let my best detractor
examine how the Greek word warrants me."   He
refers to his own commentary as affording ample
proof of his skill in the Greek tongue ; but it must
be confessed that this commentary does not give
such triumphant evidence of Chapman's scholarship
as he would have us imagine. In fact, not to put too
fine a point upon it, his Greek was very shaky ; and
if he could be summoned from the Elysian shades
and set down to a Moderations Homer paper, I, for
one, should tremble for the result.   Some of his
renderings are very whimsical.   The opening line
of the fourth book of the Odyssey—

οἱ δ᾽ ἷξον κοίλην Λακεδαίμονα κητώεσσαν

He translates by—

" In Lacedæmon now, the nurse of whales,
These two arrived."

and he adds a footnote "Λακεδαίμονα κητώεσσαν" which
is expounded *Spartam amplam,* or μεγάλην *magnam,*

where κητώεσσαν signifies properly *plurima cete nutrientem*. This one example will show that Chapman's translation is not always to be trusted. After finishing the Iliad he began the Odyssey, of which he completed a translation (dedicated to Robert Carr, Earl of Somerset) in 1616. Finally, in 1624, he concluded his Homeric labours by issuing " The Crown of all Homer's Works, Batrachomyomachia, or The Battle of Frogs and Mice. His Hymns and Epigrams," all which he turned into rhymed lines of ten syllables. The engraved title contains a fine portrait of Chapman.

Who can forget Keats' noble sonnet " On First looking into Chapman's Homer," where he compares himself to—

" Some watcher of the skies
When a new planet swims into his ken."

It was Coleridge who said that the translation was as truly an original poem as the " Faerie Queene"; and Charles Lamb was never tired of praising it. At the time of its appearance it was welcomed with generous applause. Dryden in the next age declared that the Earl of Mulgrave and Mr. Waller, two of the best judges, had told him they " could never read over the translation of Chapman without incredible transport," and according to Dr. Johnson Pope never translated any passage of Homer without first going through Chapman's rendering. In our own day Emerson, and later Mr. Swinburne, have warmly praised the rough old translation. The first thing that strikes one about Chapman's Homer is what Lamb aptly calls its " unconquerable quaintness," but we must not expect to find in it the radiant simplicity of the old poet. In his original poetry Chapman's style bristled with harsh conceits, which were the last things wanted in a translation

56

of Homer. But the translation—I speak particularly
of the Iliad—is inspired with such heat and energy,
the long fourteen-syllabled lines sweep at such a
pace that we pass lightly over the rough ridges and
are only occasionally sensible of the jolting. His
Homer was the work in which he took the most
pride. When he reached the end—" the end of all
the endless works of Homer " as he puts it—before
laying down his pen he wrote a few lines by way of
postscript : they begin " The work that I was born
to do is done." He was convinced that his translation
would live ; and live it will, though not with a
large fulness of life.

Now to come back to the plays. About 1598-9
there is a break in Chapman's dramatic career. An
anonymous comedy " Sir Giles Goosecap," written
about 1601 and printed in 1606, is so strongly marked
with Chapman's mannerisms that we may be sure it
was written in part by him if not altogether. In the
excellent comedy " Eastward Ho," 1605, he was
assisted by Jonson and Marston, but I take the play
to be in great part by Chapman. For introducing
some satirical reference to Scotch adventurers the
playwrights, at the instance of Sir James Murray,
were committed to prison ; and the report ran that
their ears were to be cut and their noses slit. Ben
Jonson told Drummond that he had not contributed
the objectionable matter, but that Chapman and
Marston " had written it amongst them." Scotch
pride seems to have been quick to take offence, for
the satirical passages—there are only two that
could give any annoyance, and one of these is suppressed in most of the printed copies—are not
outrageous. The suppressed copy runs thus : " You
shall live freely there [in Virginia] without sergeants,
or courtiers, or lawyers, or intelligencers, only a few
industrious Scots, perhaps, who indeed are dispersed

over the face of the whole earth. But as for them
there are no greater friends to English men and
England, when their out on't in the world than
they are. And for my part I would a hundred
thousand of 'em were there, for we are all one
countrymen now, ye know ; and we should find ten
times more comfort of them there than we do here."
Englishmen were disgusted, and rightly disgusted,
at the favours showered on the Scots by James ; and
it seems hard that Chapman and Marston should not
have been able to have even this little fling without
being laid by the heels.

The passage that probably gave Murray more
annoyance was a slight hit in the first scene of the
fourth act :—

> " ' I ken the man weel : he's one of my thirty
> pound Knights.' 'No, no, this is he that stole his
> knighthood o' the grand day for four pound
> giving to a page ; all the money in's purse, I wot
> wel.' "

Sir James Murray was one of those newly-created
knights, and seems from this passage to have procured
the honour—if honour it could be called—by some
underhand means ; but at this time of day we
cannot precisely tell where the sting came in. It is
satisfactory to know that Chapman and his associates
were released without suffering much inconvenience.
"Eastward Ho" is one of the best comedies that
we possess dealing with city life, a rich, racy, genial
play, and Hogarth is said to have drawn from it the
plan of his prints of the Industrious and Idle Pren-
tices. In 1606 Chapman published a comedy "The
Gentleman Usher," which contains some love-
passages of great beauty. To the same year belongs
"Monsieur d'Olive," of which the opening scenes
are very effective. From an elaborate speech in the

second act we learn that Chapman appreciated the virtues of that most valuable and beneficent of all plants, "the gentleman's saint and the soldier's idol," tobacco.

In 1607 was published the first edition of Chapman's most popular play, the tragedy of "Bussy d'Ambois," which was republished in 1608, 1616, 1641 (the text "corrected and amended by the author before his death"), and 1657. Dryden, in the dedicatory epistle before the "Spanish Friar," handles this play most severely. All that he could find in it was a "dwarfish thought dressed up in gigantic words, repetition in abundance, looseness of expression, and gross hyperboles; the sense of one line expanded prodigiously into ten; and, to sum all up, incorrect English, and a hideous mingle of false poetry and true nonsense." This is a pretty strong indictment, though it sounds odd from one who collaborated with Nat Lee; but "Bussy d'Ambois," turgid and heavy as it was, essentially undramatic, held the stage for years and years. The same indomitable energy that sweeps the reader along through Chapman's Homer held the audience spellbound in "Bussy d'Ambois." Bussy, the towering braggart, whose self-confidence knows no bounds, is an impressive personage—whatever criticism may say; and in the hands of those considerable actors Nathaniel Field, Hart, and Mountford, he appeared to the fullest advantage. It cannot be denied that the play is stuffed with bombast; but on the other hand we must be wilfully blind (as Dryden was) or critically incompetent if we fail to appreciate the extraordinary power that marks much of the writing. The best things in the play have been picked out by Charles Lamb in his "Specimens of Dramatic Poets" and his extracts from the Garrick plays. Here are some magnificent lines, an invocation for secrecy:

" Now all the peaceful regents of the night,
  Silently-gliding exhalations,
  Languishing winds and murmuring falls of waters,
  Sadness of heart and ominous secureness,
  Enchantments, dead sleeps, all the friends of rest,
  That ever wrought upon the life of man,
  Extend your utmost strengths; and this charmed
    hour
  Fix like the Centre ; make the violent wheels
  Of Time, and Fortune stand ; and great existence
  (The Maker's treasury) now not seem to be,
  To all but my approaching friend and me."

Such verse as this is not to be had for the asking ; it is poetry of the very first order. Finer still is this other invocation, to Light and Darkness.

" Terror of darkness : O thou king of flames
  That with thy music-footed horse dost strike
  The clear light out of crystal, on dark earth ;
  And hurl'st instructive fire about the world :
  Wake, wake the drowsy and enchanted night
  That sleeps with dead eyes in this heavy riddle ;
  Or thou, great Prince of Shades, where never sun
  Sticks his far-darted beams, whose eyes are made
  To shine in darkness, and see ever best
  Where sense is blindest, open now the heart
  Of thy abashed oracle, that, for fear
  Of some ill it includes, would fain lie hid,
  And rise thou with it in thy greater light."

One can easily imagine that such magnificent verse, spoken by a great actor, could not fail to stir any audience ; but, unhappily, along with this noble poetry we find much balderdash. If, however, the play contained nothing more than those two invocations it would deserve a less severe censure than

Dryden passed upon it. A Second Part—" The
Revenge of Bussy d'Ambois "—appeared in 1613 ;
it is as undramatic as the first part, rather more so ;
but it displays to advantage Chapman's copiousness
of moral and didactic reflections.

In 1608 were published together the two parts of
" The Conspiracy and Tragedy of Charles, Duke of
Byron." They had been produced on the stage as
early as 1605, and at their first production contained
some passages that gave offence to the French
ambassador, who obtained permission for the performances to be discontinued. When the Court
removed from London the players, ignoring the
injunction, persisted in presenting the piece ; whereupon three members of the company were arrested,
but the principal person, the author, escaped. The
objectionable matter must, however, have been
cancelled when the plays were put to press, for in
their present form we find nothing that could have
affronted the most hypersensitive of patriots. In
the " Conspiracy and Tragedy of Byron " there is
no dramatic movement, no development of character,
no pretence of a plot. The figure of Byron, just such
another magnificent, vainglorious boaster as Bussy
d'Ambois, is directly imposing in the " wild enormities " (to borrow an expression from Sir Thomas
Browne) of his far-reaching ambition. But the
whole tone of these plays is more epic than dramatic.
Here is a simile, one of many, fine enough in its
way, and excellently suited for epic purposes, but
quite out of place in a play :—

" And as a savage boar that (hunted long,
   Assailed and set up) with his only (?) eyes
   Swimming in fire, keeps off the baying hounds ;
   Though sunk himself, yet holds his anger up
   And snows it forth in foam ; holds firm his stand

Of battalous bristles, feeds his hate to die
And whets his tusks with wrathful majesty,
So fares this furious duke."

Charles Lamb declared that of all the English
dramatists Chapman came nearest to Shakespeare
" in the descriptive and didactic, in passages which
are less purely dramatic." In reading " Byron " and
" Bussy d'Ambois " no one can fail to notice the
many striking aphorisms so eloquently expressed, or
to see the force of the compliment that Webster
paid to Chapman in the Address to the Reader prefixed to the " White Devil," when he praised " the
full and heightened style of Master Chapman."
Chapman's next play was " May Day," published
in 1611, a comedy of broad humour full of comical
situations ; doubtless it came as a relief after the
heavy tragedies. In the next year was published
" The Widow's Tears " ; a comedy of intrigue,
vigorously written but coarse in tone, a libel on
women. The plot was partly founded on the well-
known story of the Ephesian widow in Petronius.
For several years afterwards Chapman published no
other play. At length, in 1631, appeared " Cæsar
and Pompey : A Roman Tragedy," with a dedicatory
epistle to the Earl of Middlesex, from which we
learn that the play had been written several years
before the date of publication. There is little
dramatic power in " Cæsar and Pompey," but it
exhibits in no small degree Chapman's depth of
ethical reflection. No other plays of Chapman were
published during his lifetime ; but in 1654 Hum-
phrey Moseley, who did good service in printing
from MS. some Elizabethan plays that would otherwise have been lost, published " The Tragedy of
Alphonsus, Emperor of Germany," a play that he
attributed to Chapman. It is a singularly unattractive

piece of work, brutal and bloody, but interesting (in a limited sense) from the intimate knowledge that the author displays of German manners and the German language—a language seldom studied by Englishmen in those days. I do not for a moment suppose that Chapman was the author. In the same year, 1654, the publisher, Richard Marriot, issued "Revenge for Honour," another very sanguinary drama, with a plot more regular than we find in Chapman's undoubted tragedies. Internal evidence would lead us to suppose that Marriot was not well advised in stating this play to be Chapman's. A comedy entitled "The Ball," licensed in 1632, was published in 1639 as the joint work of Chapman and Shirley ; but it may be doubted whether Chapman had any hand in it. In Sir Henry Herbert's Diary (Herbert was the Master of the Revels, the licenser of plays) it is described as written by Shirley, and is an agreeable comedy of manners. Another play, "The Tragedy of Chabot, Admiral of France," licensed on 29 April, 1635, was printed in the same year as "The Ball," with the names of Chapman and Shirley on the title-page. This play has little of the turgidity of "Bussy d'Ambois" or "Byron," so we may suppose Chapman left it imperfect and that it was finished by Shirley, who has softened the harshness and lightened the obscurities of Chapman's style. An anonymous play of considerable power, the "Second Maiden's Tragedy," licensed on the 31st October, 1611, and first printed (from an MS. in the Lansdowne collection in the British Museum), has been attributed on no sure authority to Chapman ; its authorship remains a mystery. A very ridiculous piece, "Two wise men and all the rest Fools ; or a comical Moral censuring the follies of this age," 1619, has been given by Gerard Langbaine in his "Dramatic Poets" to Chapman, but Langbaine candidly says,

" I am led only by tradition to believe this play to be his." Probably the error arose from some confusion of the title, " Two wise men and all the rest Fools," with the title of Chapman's comedy " All Fools."

So much for the plays. Now to turn back to the poems. Among the " divers poetical essays on the Turtle and Phœnix," printed at the end of Chester's " Love's Martyr," 1601, is a short poem by Chapman, " Peristeros, or the Male Turtle." It is companioned by Shakespeare's " Phœnix and Turtle," and by poems on the same subject of Marston and Ben Jonson. Shakespeare's " Phœnix and Turtle " is not easy reading, but it is clear as crystal compared with Chapman's " Peristeros." In 1609 appeared "Euthymiae Raptus, or the Tears of Peace," dedicated to Prince Henry. It is an allegorical poem, and the allegory is somewhat confused ; but the Vision of Homer in the *Inductio* is in Chapman's noblest style, and the *Conclusio* contains one passage of rich imagery and faultless harmony :—

" Before her flew Affliction, girt in storms,
  Gashed all with gushing wounds, and all the forms
  Of bane and misery frowning in her face ;
  Whom Tyranny and Injustice had in chase ;
  Grim Persecution, Poverty and Shame ;
  Detraction, Envy, foul Mishap and lame
  Scruple of Conscience ; Fear, Deceit, Despair ;
  Slander and Clamour that rent all the air ;
  Hate, War, and Massacre ; uncrownèd Toil
  And Sickness, t' all the rest the base and foil,
  Crept after, and his deadly weight trod down
  Wealth, Beauty, and the glory of a crown.
  These ushered her far off ; as figures given
  To show these crosses born make peace with heaven.
  But now, made free from them, next her before,

Peaceful and young, Herculean silence bore
His craggy club ; which up aloft he hild,
With which, and his forefinger's charm he stilled
All sounds in air, and left so free mine ears
That I might hear the music of the spheres
And all the angels singing out of heaven,
Whose tunes were solemn as to Passion given,
For now that Justice was the happiness there
For all the wrongs to Right inflicted here.
Such was the Passion that Peace now put on ;
And on all went ; when suddenly was gone
All light of heaven before us ; from a wood,
Whose sight foreseen now lost, amazed we stood,
The sun still gracing us ; when now, the air
Inflamed with meteors, we discovered fair
The skipping goat ; the horse's flaming mane ;
Bearded and trained comets ; stars in wane ;
The burning sword ; the firebrand-flying snake ;
The lance ; the torch ; the licking fire ; the drake ;
And all else meteors that did ill forebode.
The thunder chid, the lightning leapt abroad ;
And yet when Peace came in all heaven was clear ;
And then did all the horrid wood appear,
Where mortal dangers more than leaves did grow,
In which we could not one free step bestow
For treading on some murdered passenger
Who thither was by witchcraft forced to err,
Whose face the bird hid that loves humans best,
That hath the bugle eyes and rosy breast
And is the yellow autumn's nightingale."

This description of robin redbreast in the closing
lines is the best that I know, though Donne, too,
has a quaint line about the robin ; he calls him " The
household bird with the red stomacher."

In 1612 Chapman published " Petrarch's Seven
Penitential Psalms paraphrastically translated, with

other philosophical poems, and a Hymn to Christ upon the Cross " : some of these shorter philosophical poems are tense and weighty. On 6 November, 1612, Chapman's patron, Prince Henry of Wales, died, and the poet lamented his death in an " Epicede or Funeral Song." The marriage of Robert Carr, Earl of Somerset, to the divorced wife of the Earl of Essex was celebrated on 26 December, 1613, and Chapman composed in honour of the occasion an allegorical poem, " Andromeda Liberata, or the Nuptials of Perseus and Andromeda." A more extraordinary performance it would be difficult to find. The allegory was most unhappily chosen, but Chapman seems to have had not the slightest suspicion that there was anything amiss. He defended his allegory in a tract entitled " a Free and offenceless justification for a Lately Published and most maliciously misinterpreted poem," wherein he protested that he had not thought it possible that the allegory could be regarded " as intended to the dishonour of any person now living." There had been a rumour that he was subjected to personal chastisement for his indiscretion ; and he gave an indignant denial to it : " their most unmanly lie both of my baffling and wounding, saying ' Take this for your Andromeda,' not being so much as touched." It is a mysterious affair, but we need not regret that in the lives of many of the Elizabethans there is still some mystery left ; something to inflame our fancy, pique our curiosity, and leave the figures on the canvas all the more attractive because the outlines are not too sharply defined. This is an age of investigation ; of digging out the secrets dead men had hoped should perish with them ; of peeping as it were into locked rooms and turning over papers never meant for our eyes to see. I do not think on the whole that we are greatly advantaged by this vulgar though possibly natural curiosity. Like the stained glass in our old cathedral windows (to which the dust of time has given that mellowed light we sometimes wrongly attribute to the cunning of the old glass-workers), so these lives, but imperfectly known, of the poets and the playwrights are decked by our imagination with colours made all the livelier from the very poverty of our knowledge : we may lose more than we can hope to gain when, if ever, painstaking students shall have brushed away all the cobwebs.

Ben Jonson told Drummond that " next himself only Fletcher and Chapman could make a masque." I have never understood what Jonson meant by this assertion. We have only one printed specimen of Chapman's talents as a masque-writer in the " Memorable Masque of the Two Honourable Houses or Inns of Court, the Middle Temple and Lincoln's Inn," 1614, written for the Princess Elizabeth's nuptials and performed at Whitehall, and it certainly affords very slender proof of Chapman's ability for masque-writing. Had Ben Jonson said that only Fletcher and Campion could write masques the remark would have been at least intelligible. But perhaps Drummond mistook Jonson ; the names Chapman and Campion being somewhat similar in sound. In the same year (1614) Chapman published " Eugenia," a funeral poem on William, Lord Russell ; it is a tedious piece but relieved by a few touches of poetry. In 1616 appeared (with a dedication to Inigo Jones) " The divine poem of Musaeus. First of all Bookes. Translated According to the Originall, By Geo. Chapman." The Elizabethan age was not a critical age, and this poem of the pseudo-Musaeus—on the subject of Hero and Leander —was regarded as the genuine work of the ancient Musaeus. Only two copies of the translation are known, and one is in the Bodleian. It is a curious little book, measuring two inches in length and scarcely an inch in breadth ; but it is a good deal larger than the 1604 edition of Peele's " Tale of Troy," which is only an inch and a half high and not more than half an inch broad. The translation of Musaeus was followed in 1618 by a vigorous translation of Hesiod ; this Chapman dedicated to Bacon, and Michael Drayton and Ben Jonson prefixed commendatory verses. Four years later, in 1622, when Sir Horace Vere was shut up in Mannheim with a handful of troops, Chapman published a spirited poem, " Pro Vere Autumni Lacrimae," in which he urged that aid should be sent to the relief of the distressed garrison. The poem was dedicated to Robert Carr, Earl of Somerset, who had been dismissed from court and was now living in obscurity ; and however deep may be our contempt for Somerset we cannot but admire Chapman for remaining true to his fallen patron. In 1629 came the last of Chapman's writings, a very odd piece of prose, " A justification of a strange action of Nero in burying with a solemn funeral one of the cast hairs of his mistress Poppœa," to which was appended a translation—and a very lively rendering—of Juvenal's fifth satire.

Chapman died in the parish of St. Giles in the Fields on the 12th of May, 1634, and was buried in St. Giles' Churchyard ; the monument erected to his memory is still standing. Habington, in his " Castara," 1635, refers to the fact of Chapman's grave being outside the church, and expresses the hope that some person would be " so seriously devote to poesy " as to remove his relics and " in the warm church to build him up a tomb."

Anthony Wood describes Chapman as " a person of most reverend aspect, religious and temperate, qualities rarely meeting in a poet." It may be gathered from many passages in his works that he was not too amply blessed with worldly goods. John Davies of Hereford, in " The Scourge of Folly," 1611, refers to his straitened circumstances in a quaint copy of verses addressed to " my highly valued Mr. George Chapman, father of our English poets." Ben Jonson was deeply attached to Chapman, and told Drummond that " Fletcher and Chapman were loved of him,"—but the friendship suffered some interruptions. Oldys states that in his later days Chapman was " much resorted to by young persons of parts as a poetical chronicle ; but was very choice whom he admitted to him, and preserved in his own person the dignity of poetry which he compared to a flower of the sun, that disdains to open its leaves to the eye of a smoking taper."

In one of his plays Chapman speaks of men

" That have strange gifts of nature but no soul
    Diffused quite through to make them of a piece."

The description might well be applied to himself. His gifts were indeed strange, but the controlling sanity, that should have made them of a piece, was lacking.

Thomas Dekker

Thomas Dekker

OUR knowledge of the lives of the Elizabethan dramatists is usually very scanty. We gather that most of them lived and died poor, and that is often nearly all we know about them. Samuel Daniel, it is true, was admitted to the society of the noblest in the land, and by the generous help of his powerful friends was able to devote himself with composure to the pursuit of literature. Very different was the lot of Thomas Dekker. He numbered no great lords or ladies among his acquaintance; no country-houses welcomed him as an honoured guest. His life seems to have been one long strenuous struggle with poverty, a fact which should be borne in mind when we attempt to judge his achievements. He was harassed by printers' devils and sheriffs' officers; and not infrequently he was lodged in the Counter, a prison in the Poultry for debtors, where it was difficult to carry on literary work with any degree of comfort or satisfaction. But " your merry heart goes all the way," and even in the dusk and gloom of the Counter Dekker's cheeriness never deserted him. His own sufferings quickened his pity for the sorrows of others; and by no poet or divine has the worth of patience been so touchingly described as in this thrice-noble utterance of Dekker :—

> " Patience, my lord : why 'tis the soul of peace :
> Of all the virtues 'tis nearest kin to heaven,
> It makes men look like gods. The best of men
> That e'er wore earth about him was a sufferer,
> A soft, meek, patient, humble tranquil spirit,
> The first true gentleman that ever breathed."

Much may be forgiven to the writer of those lines.

Dekker's birthplace was London, as he intimates in " The Seven Deadly Sins," 1600, and " A Rod for Runaways," 1625. In 1637, in the preface to his " English Villainies," he speaks of his " three-score years " ; and if the passages could be taken literally the date of his birth would be 1577—but 1570 would probably be nearer the mark (the expression three-score years being used in a somewhat elastic sense). Already in 1628 he described himself as an old man ; and in 1631, dedicating his tragi-comedy " Match me in London " to Ludowick Carlell, a younger dramatist, he writes : " I have been a priest in Apollo's temple many years, my voice is decaying with my age." The name Dekker—variously spelled Dikker, Dekkar, Decker, Dicker, and so on—is a very uncommon English name ; and it has been suggested that the dramatist had some Dutch blood in his veins. He certainly had some knowledge of Dutch ; but it would be rash to infer that he was of Dutch origin. A " Thomas Dycker," styled " gent.," had a daughter Dorcas christened at St. Giles', Cripplegate (near the Fortune Theatre), on the 27th of October, 1594, and from the same register it appears that Anne, daughter of " Thomas Dekker, yeoman," was baptised in October, 1602. In spite of the discrepancy in the descriptions " gent." and " yeoman," the entries doubtless refer to the same person. A daughter Elizabeth and a son Thomas were buried in 1598. Collier assumed that all these were children of our Thomas Dekker, the dramatist ; and the view is plausible, though we cannot speak with certainty.

The first direct notice that we find of Dekker is in Henslowe's Diary under date 8 January, 1597-8, when he received from Henslowe, the manager, the sum of twenty shillings as part payment for an unnamed play. A week later Henslowe paid £4 " to bye a boocke of Mr. Dicker called Fayeton." This " Phaethon " was probably the play published long afterwards, in 1656, under the title of the " Sun's Darling," with the names of Dekker and Ford on the title-page, Ford having recast this early work of Dekker. In the following month Dekker was confined in the Counter for debt, and Henslowe advanced forty shillings to have him discharged. The Diary records the titles of eight plays written by Dekker single-handed between 1598 and 1602 ; and of many others in which he had a share. [In my article on Dekker in the "Dictionary of National Biography " a full list is given of the titles of the plays that he wrote at this time with his own hand or in company with other playwrights.] Of the eight plays written single-handed between 1598 and 1602 only two have come down, " The Shoemaker's Holiday, or the Gentle Craft," and " Old Fortunatus," both written in 1599 and both published in 1600. They are two of the best of Dekker's works and rank with the choicest comedies of the Elizabethan age. The " Shoemaker's Holiday " is dedicated to no highly placed patron, but " to all good fellows, professors of the gentle craft of what degree soever," and the epistle concludes with these words : " Take all in good worth that is well intended, for nothing is purposed but mirth ; mirth lengtheneth long life, which, with all other blessings, I heartily wish you. Farewell." Mirth there is in abundancy, frank, honest, hearty mirth. Simon Eyre, the humorous shoemaker, who becomes Lord Mayor of London, is a prince of good fellows, just such another jovial, rollicking madcap as Master Merrythought in the " Knight of the Burning Pestle." A graceful love-story (which ought to please the ladies) runs through the play. " Old

Fortunatus "—which was perhaps founded on an earlier piece—amply justifies Charles Lamb's remark that "Dekker had poetry enough for anything." Here he allowed his fancy to run riot. Fortunatus is offered by the goddess Fortune a choice of six things—

" Wisdom, Strength, Health, Beauty, Long Life and Riches."

He chooses riches and receives from Fortune an inexhaustible purse :

" Thou shalt spend ever and be never poor :
    For proof receive this purse, with it this virtue :
    Still when thou thrust'st thine hand into the same,
    Thou shalt draw forth ten pieces of bright gold
    Current in any realm where then thou breath'st :
    If thou canst dribble out the sea by drops
    Then shalt thou want : but that can ne'er be done,
    Nor this grow empty."

Perchance these lines were written when Dekker was lying in the Counter, waiting for some friendly hand to procure his release by advancing him two or three pounds.

On the 30th of January, 1599 (in which year the play was written), Henslowe paid three pounds ten shillings " to discharge Thomas Dickers from the arrest of my Lord Chamberlain's men "—Dekker having probably received an advance from the Lord Chamberlain's company of actors, for some play which he had failed to supply. With what gusto he sings, in the person of Fortunatus, the praises of gold !

" Gold is the strength, the sinews of the world,
    The health, the soul, the beauty most divine ;
    A mask of gold hides all deformities ;
    Gold is heaven's physic, life's restorative ;

O therefore make me rich ! not as the wretch
That only serves lean banquets to his eye ;
Has gold, yet starves ; is famished in his store :
No, let me ever spend, be never poor."

Carrying this wondrous purse, Fortunatus, pranked
in all his bravery, visits the courts of Asia and
banquets with Prester John and the Cham of Tartary.
He comes at last to Babylon, where he is welcomed
by the Soldan, who shows him the magical wishing-
cap which can transport the wearer to whatever part
of the world he may choose. Donning the cap,
Fortunatus—before the Soldan can interfere—is back
in his native Cyprus, where he tells the story of his
travels to his sons, Ampedo and Andelocia—of how
he " has revelled with kings, danced with queens,
dallied with ladies ; worn strange attires ; seen
fantasticoes ; conversed with humorists ; been
ravished with divine raptures of Doric, Lydian, and
Phrygian harmonies ; spent the day in triumph and
the night in banquetings." Sober reason is staggered
as we contemplate Fortunatus in the height of his
pride :—

" In these two hands do I gripe all the world :
This leather purse, and this bald woollen hat
Make me a monarch : here's my crown and sceptre:
In progress will I now go through the world."

And at this moment the goddess Fortune appears,
upbraids him for abusing her gift, and tells him that
the destinies deny him longer life. " I am but now
lifted to happiness," pleads Fortunatus ; " And
now I take most pride to cast thee down," says
Fortune. Fortunatus dies, and Dekker then proceeds to deal with the history of Fortunatus's sons,
who inherit the purse and the wishing-cap. Dekker
was not a great artist, and he usually showed a reckless indifference in the management of his plots. He

worked hastily, and had not the time—perhaps we should say, too, the ability—to conduct his plays with patience and orderliness. "Old Fortunatus" has the appearance of being made up of two separate plays. Yet in spite of its artistic defects it is a most attractive piece of work. The story of the inexhaustible purse and of the wishing-cap is as old as the pyramids ; but the wealth of fanciful poetry here lavished with so bountiful a hand is all of Dekker's own.

Dekker's next play was "Satiromastix, or the Untrussing of the Humorous Poet," 1602, a satirical attack on Ben Jonson. It is not easy to learn how this famous quarrel arose. In August, 1599, the two playwrights wrote together a domestic tragedy (which has not come down), "Page of Plymouth," and in the September of the same year they were engaged upon a chronicle-play, "Robert the Second." That they had quarrelled before the publication (in 1600) of "Every Man out of his Humour" and "Cynthia's Revels" is certain, for both plays undoubtedly contain satirical reflections on Dekker. The quarrel culminated in 1601 when Dekker and Marston (under the names of Demetrius Fannius and Crispinus) were unsparingly ridiculed in the "Poetaster." Demetrius is there described as a "dresser of plays about the town here"—*dresser* being synonymous with *decker*—"his doublet's a little decayed" (an ungenerous sneer at Dekker's poverty), "he is otherwise a very simple, honest fellow, sir." In the apology at the end of the play Jonson declares that for three years past he had been provoked by his opponents "with their petulant styles on every stage" ; but we have no means of deciding who was the original aggressor. "Satiromastix," which was Dekker's reply, vigorous but good-tempered, to the "Poetaster," is a strange medley of incongruities

Thomas Dekker

even for Dekker. The satirical portions harmonise
so ill with the romantic part that, as Mr. Swinburne
says, " it is impossible to regard them as component
factors of the same original plot." It is a plausible
conjecture that Dekker had begun the composition
of a serious play on the subject of William Rufus and
Sir Walter Tyrrel before the appearance of the
" Poetaster "; that he changed his plan, hastily
stitched in the satirical and farcical matter, and
so produced this odd gallimaufry. Dekker never
republished " Satiromastix "; but Jonson included
the " Poetaster" among his works in 1616, and told
Drummond of Hawthornden, in 1619, that Dekker
was a knave.

In 1603 Dekker published a prose tract " The
Wonderful Yeare, wherein is shewed the picture of
London lying sicke of the Plague," a very vivid
piece of description, which I suspect was well
known to Defoe. Like William Bullein, who gave a
living picture of the pestilence of 1563, Dekker
tempers his gruesome account of the horrors of the
plague with amusing anecdotes; for the book (as
was the earlier work of Bullein) was partly written
with the object of enlivening people's spirits during
the season of the awful visitation. In the same year
appeared " The Bachelor's Banquet," a prose tract
republished in 1604, 1630, 1660, 1661 and 1677. It
is founded on the fifteenth-century satire " Les
Quinze Joyes du Marriage "; but the subject—the
ill-treatment of husbands by their wives—is handled
with such droll ingenuity that Dekker is entitled to
claim for his brilliant tract the merit of absolute
originality. Mr. Swinburne is the only critic, so far
as I know, who has done justice to the " Bachelor's
Banquet," which he declares—and, I believe, rightly
—gives Dekker " a high place for ever among
English humorists." There are fourteen chapters,

or we might say courses, to the banquet, all of them
well seasoned with wit and drollery.

The first chapter treats of " The humour of a
young wife new-married." Her husband, finding
her one day in an ill-humour, inquires the cause.
She answers petulantly, " In truth, husband, it
were to no purpose, for I know your custom well
enough ; as for my words they are but waste wind
in your ears ; for how great soever my grief is I am
assured you will but make light of it." The good
man presses her to explain what has happened. She
tells him that she has been by invitation to a neighbour's house, where she found " great cheer and no
small company of wives." All the ladies were
becomingly attired. The meanest of them was " in
her gown with trunk sleeves, her farthingale, her
turkey grogram kirtle, her taffaty hat with a gold
band "—all in the newest fashion ; whereas " I,"
says the indignant young wife, " had on my thread-
bare gown which was made me so long ago against
I was married, besides that it was now too short for
me, for it is, I remember, since it was made about
three years." It was not so much for herself as for
her husband's credit that she was concerned. What
grieved her most was that two ladies had openly
stated that it was a shame to her husband for her to
be so meanly apparelled. Well, the end is that the
husband runs deep into debt in order to gratify his
wife's extravagant whims. When she has got her
fine clothes she goes gadding abroad to every gossips'
meeting to display them : " to which cause she
also comes every Sunday to the Church, that there
she may see and be seen, which her husband thinks
she doth of mere devotion." After a time creditors
come about (Dekker knew such visitors only too
well) ; the poor man is arrested and the wife has
to doff her peacock plumes : " but heaven knoweth

in what misery the silly man doth live, being daily vexed with her brawling and scolding, exclaiming against him that all the house doth ring thereof."

Another highly amusing chapter is the sixth— "The humour of a woman that strives to master her husband." She has to be coaxed into everything ; she will not rise for breakfast, and is always indisposed when the dinner-hour comes round. One day her husband, meeting some friends abroad, asks them home to dinner and sends on word (by a messenger) to his wife in order that she may make due preparation. "Now by my faith," says she, on receiving the message, " I will not meddle in it : he thinks belike that I have nothing else to do than to drudge about to prepare banquets for his companions." She flings herself into her room and is careful to send the servants out, some one way, some another, and placidly waits the coming of her husband and his friends. In due course they arrive : the master asks one of the maids if everything is ready, who replies that her mistress is very sick. He, fuming the while, leads his friends into the hall or some other place according to his state, " but finds neither fire made nor cloth laid." He calls for one servant and another, but there comes none except some scullion or charwoman " whom his wife hath left there of purpose because she knew that they could serve to do nothing." In no amiable frame of mind he goes up to his wife, and an interesting colloquy ensues ; but she cares not a whit for all his talk, " being well assured that however she thwarts him, he will hold his hands, and in scolding she knows herself to be the better." The poor man, at his wits' end, sends abroad for provisions (some of the servants having meanwhile returned) and orders the best table-cloth to be laid and the wrought napkins to be brought ; but the table-cloth and napkins cannot be had, for they are stowed away in the linen-chest, and his wife (or so she pretends) has lost the key. And so on, and so on, through the whole delightful book. No malice or spite is intended : it is mere fun from first to last. For Dekker was no woman-hater ; it was his loving, tender hand that drew the portrait of patient Grisel in the beautiful old play (published in this very year, 1603) that he wrote with Chettle and Haughton ; and he—I doubt not—furnished those sweet studies of womanhood, Susan and Winifred, for the tragedy of " The Witch of Edmonton," written with Ford and Rowley. But here, in the " Bachelor's Banquet," he has given us for a change a gallery of shrews.

In " Patient Grisel " are two beautiful songs— " Art thou poor, yet hast thou golden slumbers ? " (quoted in the Golden Treasury and many other anthologies) and the cradle-song, " Golden slumbers kiss your eyes," which is not quite as well-known, though it ought to be, as the other.

> " Golden slumbers kiss your eyes,
>   Smiles await you when you rise ;
>   Sleep, pretty wantons, do not cry
>   And I will sing a lullaby :
>   Rock them, rock them, lullaby.

> " Care is heavy, therefore sleep you :
>   You are care, and care must keep you.
>   Sleep, pretty wantons, do not cry
>   And I will sing a lullaby :
>   Rock them, rock them, lullaby."

There is nothing sweeter than this to be found in all Blake's " Songs of Innocence," and with one accord critics have assigned these songs to Dekker ; indeed it would be ridiculous to suppose that they belonged to either of his associates, Chettle or

Haughton. In the songs of "Old Fortunatus" Dekker had shown himself to be a true lyrist : Chettle and Haughton possessed no lyrical faculty.

In 1604 appeared the first part of a play which I will call by a title that it bears in one or two of the old copies—"The Converted Courtezan." Undoubtedly it contains Dekker's most powerful and pathetic writing, but it is marred by coarseness and exaggeration. In the first part he was assisted by Middleton; the second part, published in 1630, seems to have been wholly Dekker's work. Charles Lamb, Hazlitt, Leigh Hunt, and Mr. Swinburne, have written eloquently about this play, that may perhaps be reckoned as Dekker's masterpiece : so I may be excused from saying more. Bellafront, the reformed courtezan, in all her weakness and strength, is the most living of Dekker's characters ; as honest Orlando Friscobaldo, her father, rough to outward view but human at the red-ripe of the heart, is the most lovable.

"The Seven Deadly Sinnes of London," 1606, a powerful picture of the iniquities of the metropolis, affords a notable example of Dekker's rapidity of workmanship, for it was completed in seven days, "*opus septem dierum*," as the title-page informs us. "News from Hell, brought by the Devil's Carrier," 1606, reprinted with additions in 1607 under the title of "A Knight's Conjuring done in earnest, discovered in jest," is written in imitation of "ingenious, ingenuous, fluent, facetious T. Nashe," but, apart from the purple patches, it is not of much importance. In 1606 was also issued an anonymous tract in verse, "The double P.P., a Papist in Armes," which appears to have been written by Dekker ; it is an attack on the Roman Catholics.

To 1607 belong a jest-book, "Jests to make you Merry," by T. D. and George Wilkins, and the famous "History of Sir Thomas Wyat," by Dekker and Webster ; an abridgement of the two parts of the historical play, "Lady Jane," written (as we know from Henslowe's Diary) in 1601 with Heywood, Wentworth Smith and Webster, but published in so mutilated a form that we are really unable to judge of its merits. In the same year appeared two comedies, interesting and full of life and bustle, written in conjunction with Webster—"Westward Ho" (composed in or before 1605, as there is a reference to it in the prologue to "Eastward Ho" published in that year) and "Northward Ho"; also an allegorical play of very little value, "The Whore of Babylon," setting forth the virtues of Queen Elizabeth and the malice of Rome. "The Dead Term," 1608, dedicated to Sir John Harington, is one of Dekker's hastiest pamphlets, a thing of shreds and patches. "The Belman of London : Bringing to Light the most notorious Villanies that are now practised in the kingdon," a most interesting tract that passed through three editions in 1608, is partly taken—as Samuel Rowlands, the pamphleteer (who bore no goodwill to Dekker) pointed out in "Martin Markall, Beadle of Bridewell "—from Harman's "Caveat for Cursitors," 1566-7. It gives a very elaborate account of the practices of the rogues and sharpers who infested the metropolis. At the end of "The Belman" Dekker advertised that a second part was to follow, which should bring to light "more notable enormities." This second part appeared in the same year (1608) under the title of "Lanthorn and Candlelight, or the Belman's Second Night-Walk." Two editions followed in 1609, a fourth under the title of "O per se O, or a New Cryer of Lanthorn and Candlelight," in 1612. Between 1608 and 1648 there appeared no less than eight or nine editions of this second part, all differing more or less from one another. No public or private library possesses, so far as I know, a complete series of the old editions.

Dekker's knowledge of London, and of the vagaries practised in it, was certainly extensive and peculiar. Those who want to study Elizabethan low-life will find the " Belman " and " Lanthorn and Candlelight " simply invaluable, for Dekker had examined into all the swindling dodges of his time and was familiar with all the nooks and corners of scoundreldom. He had the canting speech of thieves and beggars—"pedlar's French," as it was jocularly called—at his fingers' ends ; but we cannot imagine him giving us a " Lavengro " or a " Romany Rye." Though he knew the life of the roads and of those picturesque travellers, the gipsies, the " moon-men " and the horse dealers through and through, he had no sentimental admiration for them ;. he could speak their language, but he had no desire to look into their hearts. Much of this canting speech, and many of the swindles that Dekker described, still flourish. Here, for instance, is a trick often practised (in one form or another) even in these days :—

"A silly fellow in show, attired like a clown, spurns (being near some candle that stands on a stall) a paper before him, in which is wrapped up a spoon: taking up which and looking on it by the light, and making it known (by his loud talking and wondering what he hath found) that he took it up by chance, people flock about him and imagine it is a silver and gilt spoon, for it looks very fair ; but he, seeming to be an innocent coxcomb, knows not, he says, what he should do with such a gew-gaw ; whereupon everyone is catching at it and offers him money for it ; he wishes he had rather found

money than such a bawble, for he eats not his
pottage in plate ; in the end some fox, amongst
all the cubs that stand about him, whispers in his
ear, to have it from all the rest, and thrusts a
crown privily into his hand. The Jumper (the cant
name for a rascal of this sort) takes it and sneaks
away; the other gets home as fast as he can,
longing till he call his wife, all his household and
neighbours about him, to show what a pennyworth
he met with ; but the gilt spoon coming to be
tried of what metal he is made, the poor man's
money proves copper and he himself is laughed at
for a coxcomb."

Oddly enough I find no mention of the painted-
sparrow dodge, and therefore suppose that that form
of swindle must be a product of modern rascality.

In 1609 appeared a tract, " The Raven's Almanac,"
intended as a parody on the prognostications of the
almanac-makers of those days. " The Owl's Almanac,
anonymously issued in 1618, has sometimes been
ascribed to Dekker, but without authority. In 1609
also appeared the most famous of Dekker's prose-
works, " The Gull's Horn-Book," which gives a
more graphic description than can be found elsewhere, of the manners of Jacobean gallants. To
some extent it is modelled on Dedekind's " Grobianus," and Dekker himself admits that it hath " a
relish of Grobianism " : those who want to examine
farther into this matter should consult Professor
Herford's book, " Germanic Influence on Elizabethan
Literature." It had been Dekker's intention to turn
" Grobianus " into English verse, but on further
reflection he " altered the shape, and of a Dutchman
fashioned a mere Englishman." In " The Gull's
Horn-Book " he prescribes how a gallant is to conduct
himself at an ordinary, at a tavern, in the theatre,

in Paul's Walk (the fashionable lounge) and so on.
The gallant is on no account to rise before noon:
Dekker is eloquent on this point.

" For do but consider what an excellent thing
sleep is. It is so inestimable a jewel that if a
tyrant would give his crown for an hour's slumber
it cannot be bought. Yea, so greatly indebted are
we to this kinsman of death, that we owe the
better tributary, half of our life to him. And
there's good cause why we should do so; for sleep
is that golden chain that ties health and our bodies
together. Who complains of wants, of wounds, of
cares, of great men's oppressions, of captivity, whilst
he sleepeth ? Beggars in their beds take as much
pleasure as kings: can we therefore surfeit on this
delicate ambrosia, can we drink too much of that
whereof to taste too little tumbles us into a churchyard, and to use it but indifferently throws us into
Bedlam ? No, no, look upon Endymion, the
Moon's minion, who slept three score and fifteen
years and was not a hair the worse for it. Can
lying abed till noon then (being not the three
score and fifteenth thousandth part of his nap) be
hurtful ? Besides, by the opinion of all philosophers
and physicians, it is not good to trust the air with
our bodies till the sun, with his flame-coloured
wings, hath fanned away the misty smoke from the
morning and refined that thick tobacco-breath
which the rheumatic night throws abroad of purpose to put out the eye of the element, which
work questionless cannot be perfectly finished till
the sun's car-horses stand prancing on the very
top of highest noon ; so that then, and not till
then, is the most healthful hour to be stirring.
. . . In a word, midday slumbers are golden; they
make the body fat, the skin fair, the flesh plump,

delicate, and tender ; they set a russet colour on the cheeks of young women, and make lusty courage to rise up in men ; they make us thrifty both in sparing victuals (for breakfasts thereby are saved), and in preserving apparel ; for while we warm us in our beds our clothes are not worn."

At the theatre the gallant is to take his seat on the stage, light his pipe, and ostentatiously play cards before the piece begins. Whether the play is good or bad he is to rail at the author, rise in the middle of the performance with a discontented countenance, salute his fashionable acquaintances, and withdraw with as much noise as possible. If the weather is bad and he is compelled to sit the play out, then he must jeer when the most pathetic passages are being spoken, begin to whistle when a song is being sung, and make himself generally objectionable to the actors and the audience.

Two other pieces were published in 1609, a prose tract, " Work for Armourers, or the piece is broken," a medley of miscellaneous matters, and a devotional work, a collection of prayers (only one copy of which is known, and that imperfect) quaintly entitled, " Four Birds of Noah's Ark." Some of the passages are beautiful pieces of composition, simple, and earnest, and strong, with no rhetorical flourishes. You have seen how Dekker wrote in his lighter moments, and I think you should listen to him for once when he is in most serious mood. I will read the prayer for a soldier preparing for battle :—

" Arm me (O thou God of battles) with courage this day that I may not fall before my enemies. The quarrel is thine ; let the victory be thine ; tie to my sinews the strength of David that I may with a pebble-stone strike to the earth these giants that fight against thy truth. The weaker means I use, the greater shall be thy glory, if I come from the field crowned with conquest. I put no confidence, O Lord, either in the strong horse or the iron-headed spear ; the armour that must defend me is thy right arm. Be thou, therefore, this day my captain to conduct me ; let thy word be the trumpet to encourage me ; the banner of the church the colours which I follow ; the weapons which I fight with, Faith and Hope ; and the cause for which I fight, the Advancement of True Religion. Keep my hands, O my God, from playing the bloody executioners ; let pity sit upon mine eyelids even in the heat of battle, and mercy on the point of my sword when it is most ready to kill. So let me fight that whether I come off lame or sound, dead or alive, I may live or die thy soldier. Bless me, strengthen me, guide me, guard me, save me, O Thou Lord of Hosts."

That is such a prayer as Wordsworth's Happy Warrior might have uttered.

The next piece on which Dekker was engaged was the excellent comedy of the " Roaring Girl," written in conjunction with Middleton, who had doubtless the larger share in the composition. Moll Cutpurse, the heroine, was in actual life a somewhat disreputable character. Her real name was Mary Frith. She was of a riotous turn from her earliest days. Her parents put her out to service, but finding the tending of children most distasteful, she abandoned service, dressed herself as a man, and became famous as a thief and bully. She used to go about with a dog which she had very carefully trained to evil courses, and on one occasion she robbed—or is reported to have robbed—General Fairfax on Hounslow Heath, and shot him through the arm. Finally she died (about the time of the Restoration) at the advanced age of 74. Her constant habit of smoking is supposed to have conduced to her longevity, for she "suffered from a dropsy" which finally despatched her. The dramatists have toned down the objectionable traits in the virago's character. She moves in the play among rowdies without suffering the least contamination. She has the thews of a giant and the gentleness of a child. In fact she is a most attractive Amazon; and this play of which she is the heroine is one of the most spirited comedies in the English Drama. I have attempted, in the introduction to my edition of Middleton, to distinguish the scenes that appear to belong to Dekker.

" If it be not good the Devil is in it," published in 1612, a very ill-constructed tragi-comedy, is wholly by Dekker, who produced in the same year " *Troya Nova Triumphans,*" a Lord Mayor's pageant. On the title-page of a copy in the British Museum, is written after Dekker's name, " merchantailor," in an early seventeenth century hand ; but his connection with the merchant tailors' company has not been traced. " A strange horse-race," 1613, is a tract exposing the rogueries of horse-dealers ; it also touches on other forms of swindling.

From 1613 to 1616, if the assertion of the antiquary Oldys (who seldom makes a statement without having some ground for it) be true, Dekker was confined in the King's Bench Prison. He was certainly there in September 1616, for he addressed some verses from the prison on the 12th of that month to Edward Alleyn the well-known actor (who founded Dulwich College). In 1620 appeared " Dekker, his Dream, in which being rapt with a poetical enthusiasm, the great volumes of Heaven and Hell to him were opened, in which he read many wonderful things." On the title-page is a rough woodcut of a man dreaming in bed, assumably a portrait of the author. It is a very rare piece (in verse), but of little merit. In 1622 was published the "Virgin Martyr," by Massinger and Dekker. Massinger was an infinitely better artist than Dekker ; he elaborated his plots carefully, and never scamped his work. To him the construction of the piece may be safely assigned ; but there can be not the shadow of a doubt that the most beautiful scene in the "Virgin Martyr," the first scene of the second act, the colloquy between Dorothea and her guardian angel Angelo, who is disguised as a page, belongs to Dekker. Even Gifford, Massinger's strongest champion, allowed this scene to be Dekker's ; but I am not quite sure that it has not been touched here and there by Massinger's hand. In the prose-tract, " A Rod for Runaways," Dekker describes the terror caused by the plague of 1625 : you will remember that John Fletcher, the dramatist, was one of those who fell a victim. A pamphlet entitled, "Wars, Wars, Wars," 1628, is so rare that nobody of the present day appears to have seen it. The late Mr. Collier was acquainted with it, for he has given some extracts from it in his Bibliographical Catalogue. For 1628 and 1629 Dekker wrote the Mayoralty pageants, " Britannia's Honour " and " London's Tempe." " Match me in London," a tragi-comedy, was published in 1631, but it must have been much older, for it is mentioned in 1623 by Sir Henry Herbert, Master of the Revels, as an " old play " that had been licensed by his predecessor, Sir George Buc.

" The Wonder of the Kingdom," a tragi-comedy, 1636, contains some brilliant writing. Jacomo Gentili, the bountiful lord who spends all the stores of his wealth in entertaining his poorer neighbours, is a striking figure. Contrasted with him is Signior Torrenti, who is all for magnificent living. Here is the description that he gives of how his house is to be fitted up :—

> " the richest hangings
> Persian, or Turk, or Indian slaves can weave
> Shall from my purse be bought at any rates ;
> I'll pave my great hall with a floor of clouds,
> Wherein shall move an artifical sun,
> Reflecting round about me golden beams,
> Where flames shall make the room seem all afire ;
> And when 'tis night, just as that sun goes down,
> A silver moon shall rise, drawn up by stars,
> And as that moves, I standing in her orb,
> Will move with her, and be that man i' the moon
> So mocked in old wives' tales ; then overhead
> A roof of woods, and forests full of deer,
> Trees growing downwards, full of singing quires ;
> And this I'll do that men with praise may crown
> My fame for turning the world upside down."

I should mention that some of the best passages in this play are found in John Day's " Parliament of Bees," published in 1641, a point of interest that had passed unnoticed until I drew attention to it in my edition of the works of John Day, published in 1881. If any reader will take the trouble to compare Day's play with Dekker's " Wonder of a Kingdom," he will find that one writer has " conveyed " much of the work of the other. The Quarto of 1641 is the only edition extant of the " Parliament of Bees," but there is a contemporary transcript, differing in many particulars from the printed copy. Dekker's play was entered on the Stationers' Register in May 1631, and was published in 1636, but the day of publication does not necessarily afford any proof of the date of composition. It must, however, be remembered that Dekker and Day had " collaborated " on more than one occasion, and it is open to a generous critic to assume that one of the two writers put his work whole-handedly at the disposal of the other.

The " Sun's Darling," more a masque than a play, printed in 1656 but licensed by Sir Henry Herbert in 1624, may be—as I said—an alteration by Ford of Dekker's lost " Phaeton." To Dekker may be safely assigned the lyrical portions, which are frequently good, whereas Ford's lyrics can hardly be praised. From Herbert's Diary we learn that Dekker wrote, in 1624, two unpublished plays with Ford, "The Bristowe Merchant" and "The Fairy Knight." " The Witch of Edmonton," published in 1658, was probably written about 1621-2, shortly after the execution of the reputed witch, Elizabeth Sawyer. I cannot discover Dekker in the powerful scenes in which Mother Sawyer figures ; those scenes I hold to be mainly by William Rowley. But Dekker, I take it—and Dekker alone, without help from his coadjutors, Ford and Rowley—drew the beautiful characters of Winifred and Susan. The poetry in this play is of the very first order. What lovelier lines could be found than these of Susan to Frank Thorney ?

> " You, sweet, have the power
> To make me passionate as an April day,
> Now smile, then weep; now pale, then crimson red:
> You are the powerful moon of my blood's sea,
> To make it ebb and flow into my face
> As your looks change."

I suspect that Tennyson remembered that passage when he made Cleopatra in " A Dream of Fair Women," say :—

" Once, like the moon, I made
The ever-shifting currents of the blood
According to my humour ebb and flow."

We last hear of Dekker in 1637 when he republished his "Lanthorn and Candlelight" with some additional matter, under the title of "English Villanies." The date of his death is unknown ; but it is probable that he died soon afterwards.

It is easy for an enthusiast to run into raptures about Dekker, and easy for a cold critic to disparage his merits ; but it is not easy to judge him fairly. We may admire him deeply, but if we are gifted with any critical power we cannot fail to notice that his work is exasperatingly faulty. In richness of imagination he was inferior to few, if any, of Shakespeare's contemporaries ; he had, too, infinite tenderness, and a vein of delightful humour. But the capacity of taking pains seems to have been wholly denied to him. Although his plays abound in passages of beauty, we can point to no piece in which he has done himself justice. Yet somehow we would not wish him to be other than he was, and he has a firmer hold on our affections than many whose names are loudly trumpeted by fame. It often happens in actual life that he by whose personality we are most deeply impressed is not the man who wins the most brilliant reputation. We see this person and that crowned with the world's applause, but we keep a very settled conviction that our poor friend in the shade, who has never attained success, really stands on a higher pedestal than these admired worthies. It may be hard for us to justify our belief, but the belief is there and will not be effaced. Some students will always have this sort of feeling towards Dekker. Criticism may pick holes in his work and belittle him ; but a few in every age will be powerfully attracted by his wayward genius.

Nicholas Breton

Nicholas Breton

NICHOLAS BRETON was a varied writer. Like so many of the Elizabethans he could turn his pen to prose or verse with almost equal skill; but it is by his verse he is now best remembered. Very sweet and gracious verse it is, though too often of most unequal merit. There is a little song of Dekker's (a single jewel set in that quaint medley " A Strange Horse-Race," 1613) that might well fit Breton's case; it runs thus :—

> " My Muse that art so merry,
> When wilt thou say thou'rt weary ?
> Never, I know it, never !
> This flight thou couldst keep ever :
> Thy shapes which do so vary
> Beyond thy bounds thee carry.
> Now plume thy ruffled wings,
> He's hoarse who always sings."

Breton's Muse was often in a jesting mood. At his best, he is light, tuneful, melodious; but anyone who has carefully read the complete edition of his works (edited by Dr. Grosart in the Chertsey Worthies' Library), must reluctantly conclude that though, at times, he could sing like a lark on a summer's morning, his notes were occasionally harsh and unpleasing. To turn out a vast quantity of verse and prose and never feel the strain is impossible : even the giants of that great Elizabethan age (and Breton cannot be reckoned as one of them) show, now and again, signs of weariness. But when all is said and done Nicholas Breton has left behind

97   H

him enough beauty to set up a dozen poets, and I hope to leave you with the sound of his music in your ears.

The Bretons came of an old Essex stock, and his father William (a younger son), went up to London and there made his fortune. At that time there were many of these young gentlemen adventurers, leaving quiet country houses to lay siege to the city, in the hope that, in their more sober years, they might become famous merchants : Hugh Clopton,— he whose " great house " Shakespeare purchased and rechristened New Place,—was himself a younger son. Dying in 1558-9, William Breton, now a rich man, bequeathed to his son Nicholas a manor in Lincolnshire, forty pounds in money, some silver spoons, and " the gilte bedsted and bedd that I lie on in London with all its furniture " ; but, by a wise provision, the boy was not to come into his inheritance until he was twenty-four years of age, and his mother was appointed his guardian. However, Elizabeth Breton (her maiden name was Bacon) had tired of widowhood before 1568, and had taken, for her second husband, George Gascoigne the poet.

Gascoigne was a versatile writer, who tried his hand (at times no light one) at almost every possible kind of literary form ; and those who are curious as to the influences that go to the making of a poet, may amuse themselves with trying to discover, in his mother's second marriage, one reason for Nicholas Breton becoming a faithful follower of the Muses. We know Breton was writing as early as 1575, and in 1577, the year of his step-father's death, he published " A Flourish upon Fancie."

The date of his birth is not known, nor is there any actual record to substantiate the tradition that he was educated at Oriel College. But he refers to

himself, in the appendix to his first published book,
as " a yong gentleman . . . who had spent some years
at Oxford," while in a contemporary diary, there
is an interesting allusion to a meeting at Antwerp
with a "Mr. Brytten, once of Oriel Colledge, w^ch
made wyts will " ; a statement that would seem to
clinch the matter.

"The Passionate Shepherd," published in 1604,
is one of the best specimens of a style of poetry very
common in Elizabethan times. It is a small collection
of " pastoral verses written by the Shepherd Bonerto
[i.e., Breton] to his beloved Shepherdess Aglaia,"
and is, to my thinking, the most attractive of all his
books. At times, it is true, we are not quite sure that
the grammatical constructions are nicely adjusted,
and meticulous critics may find the writing too
diffuse ; for Breton wrote always in haste, and
never allowed himself the luxury of revision, often
letting the rhymes carry him along and the sense
shift for itself. But in " The Passionate Shepherd "
he is in his gayest mood, and we should be churls
indeed were we not warmed by his enthusiasm and
charmed by the easy flow of his verse. The third
poem opens with a description of the joys of country
life.

> " Who can live in heart so glad
>   As the merry country lad ?
> Who upon a fair green balk
> May at pleasure sit and walk,
> And amid the azure skies,
> See the morning sun arise ;
> While he hears in every spring,
> How the birds do chirp and sing :
> Or, before the hounds in cry,
> See the hare go stealing by :
> Or, along the shallow brook,

> Angling with a baited hook,
> See the fishes leap and play
> In a blessed sunny day :
> Or to hear the partridge call
> Till she have her covey all : "

This is dainty verse.

There is always something of artificiality about pastoral poetry ; but Breton loved the country, kept open an observant eye, and so his verse has all the true ring of out-of-doors, as is shown by the quaint picture he draws us, in this same poem, of the subtle fox. Now the fox is a notable figure in much of our early literature, nor is there any sign to-day that he is in danger of losing his pride of place. But Breton writes of him simply as a fox, and does not attempt to treat his " villain " psychologically or read humanity into him : instead he tells us what he must have seen on many a country walk, but he tells it well.

> " How the villain plies the box ;
> After feeding on his prey,
> How he closely sneaks away,
> Through the hedge and down the furrow
> Till he gets into his burrow : "

Again, with what a friendly interest he watches,

> " . . . the little black-haired coney,
> On a bank for sunny place
> With her forefeet wash her face : "

Only a genuine country-lover could have given us these thumbnail sketches of country-life that are as unaffected as they are true.

Breton was very popular, and in consequence

unscrupulous publishers sometimes made free with his name. In 1591 there was published a book called "Bryton's Bowre of Delights," of which a unique copy is preserved in a private library; but its owner being a jealous guardian I have been unable to see this book. Breton distinctly states in the "Pilgrimage to Paradise" (in an address "to the Gentlemen students and Scholers of Oxforde"), that only two or three of the pieces in the collection are by him. The same statement applies to another collection, "The Arbour of Amorous Devices, by N. B. Gent" (1597 ?). There is a copy, unfortunately imperfect—the only one known—among the books that Edward Capell, the Shakespearean scholar, presented to Trinity College, Cambridge. Here is found one of the sweetest cradle-songs ever written, but we cannot be at all sure that it belongs to Breton. The man who could have written it, and perhaps did write it, was Robert Greene. Not the cradle-song of Danae by Simonides is more beautiful. It is headed "A Sweet Lullaby" and runs thus :—

" Come, little babe, come, silly soul,
 Thy father's shame, thy mother's grief,
 Born as I doubt to all our dole,
 And to thyself unhappy chief :
  Sing lullaby and lap it warm,
  Poor soul that thinks no creature harm.

" Thou little think'st and less dost know,
 The cause of this thy mother's moan,
 Thou want'st the wit to wail her woe,
 And I myself am all alone :
  Why dost thou weep ? why dost thou wail ?
  And knowest not yet what thou dost ail.

" Come, little wretch, ah, silly heart,
  Mine only joy, what can I more ?
  If there be any wrong thy smart,
  That may the destinies implore :
    'Twas I, I say, against my will,
    I wail the time, but be thou still.

" And dost thou smile ? oh, thy sweet face,
  Would God Himself He might thee see,
  No doubt thou would'st soon purchase grace,
  I know right well, for thee and me :
    But come to mother, babe, and play,
    For father false is fled away.

" Sweet boy, if it by fortune chance
  Thy father home again to send,
  If death do strike me with his lance,
  Yet mayst thou me to him commend :
    If any ask thy mother's name,
    Tell how by love she purchased blame.

" Then will his gentle heart soon yield :
  I know him of a noble mind :
  Although a lion in the field,
  A lamb in town thou shalt him find ;
    Ask blessing, babe, be not afraid,
    His sugared words hath me betrayed.

" Then mayst thou joy and be right glad ;
  Although in woe I seem to moan,
  Thy father is no rascal lad,
  A noble youth of blood and bone :
    His glancing looks, if he once smile,
    Right honest women may beguile.

" Come, little boy, and rock a-sleep,
  Sing lullaby and be thou still ;
I that can do naught else but weep,
  Will sit by thee and wail my fill :
    God bless my babe, and lullaby,
    From this thy father's quality."

Breton's devotional works in prose and verse are
not of the first quality. One of his admirers goes so
far as to compare him with Southwell and Crashaw ;
but this seems to me a mistake. The poet whom, to
my thinking, he most resembles in his religious
poems and restrained ecstasies is John Davies of
Hereford. Both Davies and Breton could spin off
any quantity of verse, and respectable verse too,
when their devotional feelings seized them, but
their devout musings exhaust one's patience at last.
The long allegorical poem, " The Pilgrimage to
Paradise," 1592, is the most readable—or the least
unreadable—of Breton's sacred poems : I will give
you two verses from it that can hardly fail to please
you :—

" Sleep is the pride of ease, the height of pleasure,
  The Nurse of nature, and the rule of rest :
  The thought's atonement, and the senses' treasure,
  The bed of love, that likes the body best :
  Against unrest the only remedy
  And only medicine to each malady.

　　.　　.　　.　　.　　.　　.

" Sleep is the soul's disease, the mind's dispight,
  The Curse of Nature, and the cross of rest :
  The thoughts' disquiet, and the darksome night,
  Wherein the spirit likes the body lest :
  A loss of time and reason's malady,
  Where death is found but sorrow's remedy."

We have all experienced, at some time or another, these two states of being, sleep that is rest, and sleep that is no rest, and it would be hard to better Breton's description of this twofold mystery of nature.

His lyrical poems are far more interesting. A short collection of these appeared in 1600 under the title of " Melancholic Humours in Verses of divers Natures," and Ben Jonson prefixed a complimentary sonnet to it. Breton is fond of playing on words and phrases, bandying them to and fro, saying the same thing in a dozen different ways, chasing a conceit about like a boy after a butterfly. It is not very exalted work, but the rhymes have a pleasant tinkle. In his " Melancholic Humours " we have some characteristic examples of his lyrical style, as in this, " Farewell to Love " :—

> " Farewell, love and loving folly,
>   All thy thoughts are too unholy :
>   Beauty strikes thee full of blindness,
>   And then kills thee with unkindness.
>
> " Farewell, wit and witty reason,
>   All betrayed by fancy's treason :
>   Love hath of all joy bereft thee,
>   And to sorrow only left thee.
>
> " Farewell, will and wilful fancy,
>   All in danger of a frenzy :
>   Love to beauty's bow hath won thee,
>   And together all undone thee.
>
> " Farewell, beauty, sorrow's agent ;
>   Farewell, sorrow, patience' pageant :
>   Farewell, patience, passion's stayer ;
>   Farewell, passion, love's betrayer.

" Sorrow's agent, patience' pageant,
  Passion's stayer, love's betrayer,
  Beauty, sorrow, patience, passion,—
  Farewell, life of such a fashion.

" Fashion, so good fashions spilling ;
  Passion, so with passions killing ;
  Patience, so with sorrow wounding ;—
  Farewell, beauty, love's confounding."

There is, too, a quaint poem, " The Strange A, B, C,"
of which I will read you the first and second verses :—

" To learn the babies' A, B, C,
  Is fit for children, not for me.
  I know the letters all so well
  I need not learn the way to spell ;
    And for the cross, before the row,
    I learn'd it all too long ago.

" Then let them go to school that list,
  To hang the lip at . . . *Had I wist :*
  I never lov'd a book of horn
  Nor leaves that have their letters worn ;
    Nor with a fescue to direct me,
    Where every puny shall correct me."

Had he lived in these days, we may be sure that he
would have been attracted by the old French forms,
and have given us rondels, and virelays, in the
manner of Mr. Austin Dobson.

In " England's Helicon " we have the best of
Breton's lyrics, and very good they are. One of
them, " Phyllida and Corydon," is well-known, and
has been included in the " Golden Treasury " and
many other anthologies ; it was written in 1591 for
an entertainment given to Queen Elizabeth by the

Earl of Hertford. Michael Este, the composer, set it to music in 1604, and it is also found in Henry Youll's " Canzonets," 1618.

> " In the merry month of May,
> In a morn by break of day,
> Forth I walk'd by the wood-side,
> Whenas May was in his pride :
> There I spied all alone,
> Phyllida and Corydon.
> Much ado there was, God wot !
> He would love and she would not.
> She said never man was true ;
> He said, none was false to you.
> He said, he had loved her long ;.
> She said, Love should have no wrong.
> Corydon would kiss her then ;
> She said, maids must kiss no men,
> Till they did for good and all ;
> Then she made the shepherd call
> All the heavens to witness truth
> Never loved a truer youth.
> Then with many a pretty oath,
> Yea and nay, and faith and troth,
> Such as silly shepherds use
> When they will not Love abuse,
> Love which had been long deluded,
> Was with kisses sweet concluded ;
> And Phyllida, with garlands gay,
> Was made the lady of the May."

And here is another, a pleasant jingling ditty :—

> " Say that I should say I love ye,
> Would you say 'tis but a saying ?
> But if Love in prayers move ye,
> Will you not be moved with praying ?

" Think I think that Love should know ye,
    Will you think 'tis but a thinking ?
But if Love the thought do show ye,
    Will ye loose your eyes with winking ?

" Write that I do write you blessed,
    Will you write 'tis but a writing ?
But if Truth and Love confess it,
    Will ye doubt the true inditing ?

" No, I say, and think, and write it ;
    Write, and think, and say your pleasure ;
Love, and Truth, and I indite it,
    You are blessed out of measure."

In another poem that was not printed in any of his
works but preserved in an MS. miscellany, Breton
gives us a pretty description of love-making in the
happy days of pastoral simplicity. Whether there
ever was such a time since Eve and Adam fled
Paradise who can say, but the old poets loved to
talk about it, and Breton followed on the well-worn
track where the Greek singers had gone before him.

" In time of yore when Shepherds dwelt
    Upon the mountain rocks ;
And simple people never felt
    The pains of lovers' mocks ;
But little birds would carry tales
    Twixt Susan and her sweeting ;
And all the dainty nightingales
    Did sing at lovers' meeting.
Then might you see what looks did pass
    Where shepherds did assemble ;
And where the life of true love was
    When hearts could not dissemble.

Then yea and nay was thought an oath
   That was not to be doubted ;
And when it came to faith and troth
   We were not to be flouted.
Then did they talk of curds and cream,
   Of butter, cheese and milk :
Then was no speech of sunny beam,
   Nor of the golden silk.
Then for a gift a row of pins,
   A purse, a pair of knives ;
Was all the way that love begins ;
   And so the shepherd wives.
But now we have so much ado
   And are so sore agrieved ;
That when we go about to woo
   We cannot be believed.
Such choice of jewels, rings and chains
   That may but favour move ;
And such intolerable pains
   Ere one can hit on love ;
That if I still shall bide this life
   'Twixt love and deadly hate ;
I will go learn the country life
   Or leave the lover's state."

As a satirist, Breton had little of the " *saeva indig-
natio* " that inspired Marston and Hall, and from
his satirical or semi-satirical writings we get a truer
insight into the manners of the time than is presented by the more violent satirists. In his " Pasquil's
Madcap," 1626, he gives us a capital picture of a
humdrum country parson, such as were common in
those days though rare in these :—

" Take an odd Vicar in a village-town
   That only prays for plenty and for peace,
If he can get him but a thread-bare gown,
   And tithe a pig and eat a goose in grease,

And set his hand unto his neighbour's lease,
    And bid the clerk on Sundays ring the bell,
    He is a churchman fits the parish well."

His satire is never very pungent ; he mixed no gall
with his ink, and might have said with Ben Jonson,

"All gall and copperas from his ink he draineth,
    Only a little salt remaineth."

There was nothing ill-natured or acrimonius about
him. He looked rather at the comic than the tragic
side of life, and was concerned rather with the
foibles than the vices of mankind. He was more a
character drawer, in the manner of Earle, and
Overbury and Braithwaite, than a satirist like Marston or Hall or Donne. He is not so terse and epi-
grammatic as Overbury, but he is far more genial.
His little book, "The Good and the Bad, or a
Description of the Worthies and Unworthies of this
Age," 1616, reminds us a good deal of Fuller's
"Holy and Profane State." Indeed, Fuller seems
to have closely studied these characters of Breton,
though he has improved upon them, for he had a
richer vein of humour than Breton, a sounder and
profounder knowledge of men and things, a pithier
and weightier expression.

Yet some of Breton's phrases are worth remembering, as when he tells us, "A wise man is a clock
that never strikes but at his home, or rather like a
dial that being set right with the sun, keeps his true
course in his compass." No one will quarrel with his
description of a honest man,—"like a plain coat,
which without welt or gard keepeth the body from
wind and weather, and being well made fits him
best that wears it"; or of the quiet woman,—"like
a still wind, which neither chills the body, nor blows
dust in the face . . . she is her husband's down-bed

where his heart lies at rest." Breton has a word to
say on a vast of men ; physicians, soldiers, judges,
lawyers, usurers, kings, knights, bishops, drunkards,
fools, and many more. A coward, he tells us is " the
child of Fear. He was begotten in cold blood when
Nature had much ado to make up a creature like a
man," and a beggar is " the child of Idleness whose
life is a resolution of ease." Of the " Honest Poor
man " he writes with such deep feeling and under-
standing that I venture to quote the larger part of
this " character."

" An honest poor man is the proof of misery ;
where patience is put to the trial of her strength
to endure grief without passion in starving with
concealed necessity, or standing in the adven-
tures of charity. If he be married, Want rings
in his ears and Woe watereth his eyes. If single,
he droopeth with the shame of beggary, or dies
with the passion of penury. Of the rich, he is
shunned like infection, and of the poor learns but a
heart-breaking profession. His bed is the earth and
the heaven is his canopy, the sun is his Summer's
comfort and the moon is his Winter candle. . . .
He is a stranger in the world, for no man craves
his acquaintance and his funeral is without cere-
mony, when there is no mourning for the miss
of him ; yet may he be in the state of election
and in the life of love and more rich in grace
then than the greatest of the world."

" The Good and the Bad " was published in 1616,
the year of Shakespeare's death, but though the
conditions of modern life have blunted the wit of
some of these " characters," this picture of the
honest poor man is unhappily as true to-day as when
Breton drew it with his heart as with his pen.
One of Breton's most entertaining books is

'Fantasticks." It was published in 1626 and the dedication runs: "To the worshipped and worthy Knight, Sir Mark Ive of Rivers Hall in Essex, N.B. wishes on earth heart's ease, and heaven hereafter." As to the second part of the wish we know nothing, but the book must have given the worthy knight some pleasure, as it would readers of to-day, were they persuaded to tackle it. For "Fantasticks" is a volume of brief essays on a number of pleasant subjects, such as "The World," "Love," "Money," "The Spring," "Summer," "Harvest," "Winter," and the like. Breton takes the twelve months each in turn and gives a short description of them. There is nothing very new in what he tells us, but he has his own quaint way of putting it, as when he says of March, "Now beginneth Nature (as it were) to wake out of her sleep and send the traveller to survey the walks of the world"; of April, "It were a world to set down the worth of this month"; of May, "It is from the Heavens a grace, and to the Earth a gladness"; of August, "I hold it the world's welfare and the earth's Warming-pan"; and of November that 'tis "the discomfort of Nature and Reason's patience"; a judgment which few will dispute.

Then he sketches Christmas Day, Lent, Good Friday and Easter Day, and this is what he says of Lent—a season much more strictly observed then than now,—for butchers had to shut up shop altogether in Lent time except in some special cases.

"It is now Lent, and the poore stockfish is sore beaten for his stubbornesse: the Herring dominiers like a Lord of great Seruice, and the fruit of the Dairy makes a hungry Feast: Fasting and mourning is the life of the poore, and the Dogges grow leane, with the lacke of bones, while the Prisoners

heart is nipt with penury : the Beasts of the
Forests have a bare feed, and the hard crusts try
the teeth of the Beggar : the Byrd hath a little
shelter in the Bush, and a bitter frost makes a
backward Spring : the Sunne giues but little
warmth, and the March wind makes the Ayre
cold : the Fisher-men now are the Rakers of the
Sea, and the Oyster gapes to catch hold of the
Crab : Solitarinesse and Melancholy breed the
hurt of Nature, and the nakednesse of the Earth
is the eyes discomfort : Idle people sit picking of
sallets, and necessity of exercise is an enemy to
study : the winds grow dangerous to the Sayler and
the Rockes are the ruine of the merchant : the
Sentinell now keeps a cold watch, and the Sconce
is nothing comfortable to the Souldier : the
Shepheard hath little pleasure in his Pipe, and Age
hath but a dead feeling in loue : the Colt hath a
ragged coat, and the halfe-mewed head disgraceth
the Deere : the Faulcons wing is but young
feathered, and the deepe fallow wearies the
Huntsman : there is nothing pleasing but hope,
that the dayes will lengthen and time will be
more comfortable. I conclude, in it selfe, it is an
vncomfortable season, the Heavens frown, and
the Earths punishment. Farewell."

A cheerless picture that ; one's spirits droop at the
prospect. But Easter Day will come at last, when
this season of sorrows ended the starveling Jack-o'-
Lent will be turned out of doors, the fishermen may
hang up their nets and take their well-earned
holiday, the velvet heads of the forest fall at the
loose of the cross-bow, the salmon trout play with
the fly, the air be wholesome, the sky comfortable on
the sun's dancing day, and Earth's Holy Day.
Breton's quaint prose is a temptation to me ; I am

loath to leave it and would willingly give you some extracts from his notes on the Hours with which the book ends. But there is another of his works, " A Post with a Packet of Mad Letters," of which I must speak. It is a sort of complete letter writer, a handbook of epistolatory correspondence that was printed in 1603, and reprinted after with additions. A son can learn from it how he ought to address his father, and a lover how he should write to his mistress. There is the letter of the jealous husband to his wife and her answer ; a letter of challenge ; a letter to persuade a friend to marry, with the friend's answer ; a letter to dissuade a friend from marriage, with the answer ; a letter to a creditor, with the answer ; a letter to an unthankful person ; a letter from a yeoman in the country to his son in London ; a letter of scorn to a dame, with her answer ; a letter recommending a servant ; a letter from a father to his son at the University, and from the son to the father ; an old man's letter to a young widow ; a letter from a traveller beyond the seas to his wife in England. In fact, every variety of letter for persons of all ages and every degree. A book on a similar plan, called " The English Secretary," written by a certain Angel Day, had been published in 1586 and passed through several editions down to 1614. We will take one or two specimens of these letters of Breton's. The first is a letter of a young man to his mistress, desiring marriage : a plain, matter-of-fact epistle in which the writer comes to the point without any hesitation or shilly-shallying, but with a pleasing sincerity that carries conviction.

" Courteous Mistris *Amee*, the only joy of my heart, I thought it fitting to declare my minde in writing to you : long time haue I rested your true and constant loue, hoping to finde the like

true affection from you : I write not in any dissembling sort, my tongue doth declare my heart, assuring you that I doe not regard any portion, but your hearty loue to remaine firme to me. I will be glad to know when you would appoint the day of our marriage, if it stand so to your liking : deare *Amee*, take some pitty on him that loueth you so well : you know that I have beene profferd good mens daughters in marriage, but I could neuer fancy any so well as yourselfe. I desire to know the fulnesse of your affection, whether it doth equall mine or no, and upon the receit of your answer you shall see me shortly after : (though I receiue you in your smocke) I have sufficient meanes to provide for you and me both. I have sent you a ring in token of loue, which I pray you accept of. I omit all eloquence, not doubting but you will consider my feruent zeale which cannot be expressed with words. Thus requesting your answer, I commit you to God, resting
Your assured loving friend till death, H. K."

But for beauty of thought and language none of these " Mad Letters " can rival the answer to that " Of comfortable advice to a friend, who sorrows for the death of his Love." We all know the difficulty, almost the impossibility of writing such a letter, for the deeper our sympathy the more pen-tied we feel. But this letter of condolence to " Honest Alexander " is in the best possible taste, has a manly ring, and when the writer says " Leave thy solitary dwelling and come live with me, we will devise some good meannes for the remoue of this melancholy," we know he speaks from his heart. But hear " Honest Alexander's " answer.

" Kind *Franke*, I have received thy friendly Letter, and note thy carefull loue ; but pardon

me if I doe not answer to thy liking. Alas, how
can he truly judge of Loue, that never kindly was
in Loue ? or know how soundly to helpe a sorrow,
that never inwardly felt it ? Reading makes a
Scholler by rule, and obseruation I know doth
much in the perfection of Art, but experience is
the Mother of Knowledge. My Mistresse beauty
was no moonshine, whose vertue gave light to the
hearts eye ; nor her wisedome, an ordinary wit,
which put reason to his perfect vnderstanding :
and for her graces, are they not written among
the vertuous ? Thou saidst well, she was too
heauenly a Creature to make her habitation on this
earth : and is it not then a kind of hell to be
without her in this world ? Imaginations are no
dreames, where substances are the object of the
senses, while the eye of memory is neuer weary of
seeing. Oh, honest *Franke*, thinke thou hast not
liued that hast not loued, nor canst liue in this
world, to have such a loue die in it : It is a dull
spirit that is fed with obliuion, and a dead sense
that hath no feeling of loue : thinke therefore
what was, is with me, and my selfe as nothing
without the enjoying of that something, which
was to me all in all. Is not the presence of an
Angell able to ravish the sight of a man ? And is
not the light of Beauty the life of Loue ? Leaue
then to burthen mee with imperfection in my
sorrow for her want, whose presence was my
Paradise, and whose absence is my worlds hell :
thou dost misconstrue my good, in a languishing
for her lacke, and knowest not my heart in thinking
of any other comforts : No, *Franke*, let it suffice
though I loue thee, I cannot forget her : and
though I liue with thee, yet will I die for her :
have patience then with my passion, till time
better temper my affection : in which, most

deuoted to thee of any man liuing, till I see thee
(which shall be as shortly as I well can) I rest,

Thine, as thou knowest, D. E."

Possibly, as he read it, " Kind *Franke* " remembered
that it is not always wise to put a strong plaster on
a green wound.

Breton, as I have said, was a voluminous writer ;
from 1575 to 1626 he was busy turning out verse
and prose, and it would take a fat volume to do
him a full measure of justice. His novel, " The
Miseries of Mavillia, the most unfortunate lady that
ever lived," was published in 1599, and most certainly justifies its title. Though it was dismissed with
contempt by Dunlop (who had probably never read
it) in his " History of Fiction," I have found some
interest in following the fortunes of the ill-starred
heroine ; but I do not suppose it would be to the
taste of many readers to-day.

The most whimsical of Breton's books is his
" Crossing of Proverbs," 1616. He first gives a
proverb and then proceeds to contradict it, as thus :
" Two may keep counsel if the third be away—Not
if a woman be one." " A bird in the hand is worth
two in the bush—Not if they be fast limed." " 'Tis
merry when gossips meet—Not if they fall out about
the reckoning." Charles Lamb has done much the
same thing, but at greater length, in his fanciful and
wholly delightful " Popular Fallacies," where he
gives us a popular saying and then grinds it to
powder.

Breton has a fancy for proverbs, as is shewn in his
" Wits Private Wealth," 1612, a collection of which,
he says, " some of them were written by wiser men
than myself " ; and also an affection for dialogues,
many of his works taking this form. They are often
of the thinnest texture, merely written to introduce

a good anecdote, as in " Grimello's Fortunes," 1604, where he tells an excellent story of an eel and a magpie, that I do not remember to have seen elsewhere.

" A neighbour of mine, in good case to liue, though not verie wealthie, and yet such a one as with his formality on a Hollidaie at Church would haue bene taken for the Hedborough of the Parish : this honest, substantiall man, drawing one daie a Mill-poole, among other fish, lighted on a verie great Eele : which, hauing got on lande, hee brought into his house, and put it with small Eeles into a Cesterne, where, feeding it euery Morning and Evening, hee made (as it were) an Idoll of it. For, there passed not a daie wherein hee had not that care of his Eele, that it seemed that hee had not of greater and better matters. This Eele, being taken about Candelmas, hee meant to keepe and feede till Lent following, when hee meant to present him to his Land-lord, for a great gratulation : in the meane-time, hee neuer went out of doores without giuing warning to his wife and his servants, to looke wel to his Eele. When he came in, How doth mine Eele ? when were you with mine Eele ? who looked to mine Eele ? I charge you looke well to mine Eele. Now his wife, a iollie stout Dame, who made more reckoning of honestie than either beautie or wisdome (for she was troubled with neither) had in her house a young Pie : (which we call a *Magot-a-Pie*). This Bird, having bin hatched in a Neste hard vnder her chamber window, she chaunced to take into her education : and being one that loued to heare a tongue wagge, either her owne, her Gossips, her Maides, or her Pyes : for if one were still, the other must be walking : and

when they were all upon the going, there was no
still-piece of musique : It fell out that this Good-
wife, not a little displeased at her Goose-mans
folly in such so much care ouer the fish, that the
flesh was but a little set by : one daie (when her
Asseband was gone forth), sitting with her maide
at the wheele, so full at her heart that yet her
tongue would have swelled if it had not broke out
at her mouth, began thus to fall in hande with
her Maid-seruant : I dare not depose for her
Virginitie, but, as I said, her maide : she fell thus
to breake her minde unto. Wench, quoth she,
doest thou not see what a sturre thy maister keepes
with a scurvy Eele ? In good earnest a little thing
would make me take her out of the Cesterne, and
put her in a Pye, or eate her some waie or other :
for better haue one chiding for all then have such
a doe as we have about her. In truth, Mistresse,
quoth she (as one whose mouth hung verie fitting
for such a piece of meate), if it please you, I will
quickly ridde you of this trouble. My maister is
ridde to your Landlords, and there I know he will
tarrie to night: if it please you I will fetch her out
of the Cesterne and kill her, and flea her, and put
her in a Pye, and you may dispatch her ere he come
home, or saue a piece for him when he is quiet after
his chiding. Content, wench, quoth she, I pray
thee dispatch her quickly. I warrant you, quoth
shee, forsooth with a trice. Thus was the Eeles
death approaching, and the matter thoroughly
enacted. Now the Pye being made and baked, and
set on the Table, and betwixt the maide and her
Dame (or mistresse) brought to such a passe that
there was very litle left for her master: the
Magot-a-Pye like a vyle Bird (that would keepe
no counsaile, but duely would vse her tongue, to
talke of all that she saw or heard) no sooner saw

the good-man come into the house, but (as shee
was taught to speake), began with Welcome home,
maister : and then (more then she was taught),
she fell to pratle, Hoh maister, my Dame hath
eaten the Eele : my Dame hath eaten the Eele :
my Dame hath eaten the great Eele. The good man
remembering his fish, began now to aske his wife,
How doth mine Eele ? What meanes the Bird to
talke thus of eating the great Eele ?   Tush,
Husband, quoth she, warme you I pray you, and
goe to bed. It is cold and late, talke of your Eele
to-morrow.   No, quoth he, I will not goe to bed
till I haue seene mine Eele : and therewith in a
bodily feare of that which was fallen out, goes to
the Cesterne, and there finding his Eele gonne,
comes in againe, as dead at hart as a Stocke-fish
(and yet resolved to brawle out of reason). Comes
[Cries ?] out : Why hoh ! The good wife, ready
to burst with laughing and yet keeping it in with
a fayned sigh, sits downe in a chaire, and hangs the
head, as though she had had the mother.   The
maid hauing wit enough (to make a foole of a
tame-goose), meetes her maister, and catching him
in her armes cries out, But softly, maister, be a
man, and mooue not all.   My dame you know
loues you well, and it may be she breedes, and
[will] bring you a boye worth twenty bushels of
Eeles : saie she had a minde to it, and hath eaten
it : if you should seem to chide for it, it may be
a meane to cast her awaie, and that she goes
with : and therefore say nothing of it, let it goe.
For indeed it is gone.   Saist thou so, my Girle ?
quoth hee, I thanke thee : hold thee, there is a
Tester for thee for thy good counsaile, I warrant
thee all shall be well.   Then in a goes to his wife,
and findes her in her chaire sitting as it were
heauily : comes to her and takes her by the hand

with, How now wife ? be of good cheere, and
take no thought, much good doe thy hart with
her, take the rest that are left, if thou haue a
minde to them I pray thee. With this she (as it
were awaked out of a trance) said, I thanke you
good husband, and so after a few home-complaints,
to bed they went, where they agreed so well that
the next morning hee had his part (though it
were the least) of that was left, and glad of it too,
and so without more adoe goes about his busines.
But no sooner was he out of doores, but the
mistresse and the maid went to the bird, the *Pye*,
and taking her out of the Cage, plucked all the
feathers off from her head, and left her as bare
as a balde Coote, which in the cold winter was
very vncomfortable : which done she was put
into the Cage againe, with these wordes, Tell
tales againe of the Eele, doe.

Now about dinner time, comes in againe the
good-man, and brings in with him a neighbour of
his, with a good face, but a balde head, that he
had almost no haire on it. Now the Pye being let
out of the Cage, no sooner sees this man put off
his hat, but she skips on his shoulders and sayes :
Oh, your head hath bene puld as well as mine, for
telling of tales. You haue told my maister, how
my dame eate the great Eele : (and so she would
do to any that shee saw bald, that came into the
house.) And was not this a merrie iest of the Pye
and an Eele ? ”

In 1592-3, Breton had married Ann Sutton, and
by her had two sons and two daughters; but though
we know the dates of his children's births and his
daughters' deaths, we do not know when this light-
hearted genial tempered singer passed into the long
silence. The supposed date is 1626, when his last

book was published ; but this is not a sure guide, seeing how many a man has outlived his pen.

Well, I have given you a taste of Nicholas Breton. A man of substance, he had, we may take it, an easy life, free from the poverty and anxieties that have helped to spoil the work of so many writers, and doubtless he has given us the best there was in him to give. As a lyrist he stands alongside of Thomas Lodge ; there is a pleasant, sprightly lilt in his lyrics ; they are of the right singing quality and many of them were set to music by Elizabethan composers. There is not much to be said in favour of his long sacred and didactic poems ; but his prose, which is always quaint and neatly turned, is valuable —very valuable—for the bright, cheerful pictures that he gives of Elizabethan society.

The Elizabethan Song-Writers
Dr. Thomas Campion

Dr. Thomas Campion

FOR the subject of my lecture this afternoon I have chosen one of the Elizabethan Song-writers, one of the most rarely gifted of them all (as I venture to think), Dr. Thomas Campion. In Elizabeth's days music and song were cultivated to perfection. Everybody sang from the highest to the lowest. Old Thomas Tusser in his "Points of Huswifry" recommends farmers' wives to chose only such servants as sing at their work—

"Such servants are oftenest painful and good
That sing in their labour as birds in the wood."

To sing at sight in those days was considered a very necessary accomplishment ; and if a person professed his inability to comply he was looked upon as a very ill-conditioned fellow. Thomas Morley, the madrigal writer, in his "Discourse of Practical Music," 1597, shows what inconveniences might arise by neglecting so important a part of one's education. A young man had been out to supper. "But supper being ended," says Morley, "and music-books according to custom being brought to the table, the mistress of the house presented me with a part, earnestly requesting me to sing ; but when after many excuses I protested unfeignedly I could not, everyone began to wonder ; yea, some whispered to others, demanding how I was brought up ; so that upon shame of my ignorance I go now to seek out mine old friend, Master Gnorimus, to make myself his scholar."

The first, in order of time, of the famous Elizabethan composers was William Byrd, who was born about 1538 and died in 1623. He was successively organist of Lincoln Cathedral and Gentleman of the Chapel Royal. His earliest collection, " Psalms, Sonnets, and Songs of Sadness and Piety " appeared in the year of the Armada, 1588. In this book he gives eight reasons why people should learn to sing. Here are some of them :—

" The exercise of singing is delightful to Nature and good to preserve the health of man."

" It is a singular good remedy for a stuttering and stammering in the speech."

" It is the best means to procure a perfect pronunciation and to make a good orator."

" There is not any music of instruments whatsoever comparable to that which is made of the voices of men, where the voices are good and the same well sorted and ordered."

There is some excellent poetry in Byrd's collections, but Byrd was only responsible for the music. Some of the songs found their way into " England's Helicon," the most delightful of the old anthologies ; and by that means one or two of them have been included in Professor Palgrave's " Golden Treasury." Byrd was particularly fond of setting quaint moral verses to music ; he was of a somewhat pious turn.

Another famous composer was John Dowland, who was praised for his " heavenly touch upon the lute," in a sonnet that was long attributed to Shakespeare, but is now known to have been written by Richard Barnfield. Dowland spent much of his time abroad. About 1580, when he was twenty years of age, he started on his travels, went through " the chiefest parts of France, a nation furnished with great variety of music," settled for awhile in Germany, and visited many Italian towns, Venice, Padua, Genoa, Florence, and other places, winning fame wherever he went by his skill as a musician. On his return to England he took his degree at

Dr. Thomas Campion

Oxford as Bachelor of Music in 1588; and afterwards went to Denmark and served as lutenist to King Christian IV. He is supposed to have died about 1615, leaving a son Robert Dowland, who gained some fame as a composer. In John Dowland's song-books we find some of the richest lyrical poetry of the Elizabethan age; but there is no ground for supposing that he wrote any of the lyrics. In some instances we know the names of the writers of the words that he set to music. As a specimen of the poetry at its best I will quote the following song :—

> " I saw my Lady weep,
> And Sorrow proud to be advanced so
> In those fair eyes where all perfections keep.
> Her face was full of woe,
> But such a woe (believe me) as wins more hearts
> Than Mirth can do with her enticing parts.

> " Sorrow was there made fair,
> And Passion wise ; Tears a delightful thing ;
> Silence beyond all speech, a wisdom rare ;
> She makes her sighs to sing,
> And all things with so sweet a sadness move
> As made my heart at once both grieve and love.

> " O fairer than aught else
> The world can show, leave off in time to grieve.
> Enough, enough : your joyful look excels ;
> Tears kill the heart, believe.
> O strive not to be excellent in woe,
> Which only breeds your beauty's overthrow."

But great as are Byrd and Dowland I would claim a yet higher place for Dr. Campion, who possessed the double gift of music and poetry. In addition he was a physician of note ; he wrote some masques of

127

much grace and sweetness, a volume of Latin verse, a critical treatise (of a somewhat odd character) on English versification, and a treatise on counter-point that was considered the standard work on the subject throughout the seventeenth century. We know very little about him. That distinguished antiquary, Dr. Jessopp (who wrote his life for the Dictionary of National Biography) says that he was probably a son of Thomas Campion of Witham, Essex, who married a Chelmsford lady, Anastace Spettey. Unfortunately Dr. Jessopp forgot to consult Chester's London Marriage Licenses (and it only occurred to me recently to look up that volume). It there appears that the Thomas Campion of Witham married Miss Spettey in 1597—when our Thomas Campion the poet would be about thirty years of age.

We are in the dark about his parentage. A Thomas Campion—who was unquestionably the poet—was admitted a member of Gray's Inn in 1596. In one of his Latin epigrams he has an address to the members of Gray's Inn, from which it appears— beyond any doubt—that he was once a member of the Inn.* It also appears from his epigrams that he

* Mr. Percy Vivian (in his edition of Campion's Works, 1909) gives, at some length, the poet's pedigree, descent and early circumstances. Mr. Vivian says : " Egerton MS. 2599 was first pointed out to me by Mr. Flower, of the British Museum, but, beyond the fact that it referred to a Thomas Campion at Cambridge, I could at first find no sure footing for identification. Finally, however, a laborious search through accounts and title-deeds, Latin and English, disclosed the allusion to ' Thomas Campion de Grayes ynne.' This was the keystone to the whole structure of material. It had been shown by Mr. Bullen that the poet was a member of Gray's Inn, and the records of the Inn make it clear that it only boasted one Campion at this date. . . . I have to thank Mr. Bullen, the pioneer of the study to which I am a mere apprentice, for his assistance, and for kind permission to quote several notes from his own editions. . . . After his [Campion's] long oblivion it was Mr. Bullen who acted as a pioneer of his works, and who restored him,.

had a distaste for the legal profession. Abandoning it he applied himself to medicine, and took his degree of M.D. but whether he obtained it at home or abroad is not known. He certainly was resident for some time at Cambridge, for there is an early notice of him in that rare book " Polimanteia " 1595, the author of which—supposed to be a certain William Clerke*—addressing Cambridge, says, " I know, Cambridge, howsoever now old, thou hast some young ; bid them be chaste, yet suffer them to be witty ; let them be soundly learned, yet suffer them to be gentlemanlike qualified." Opposite this passage is a marginal note " Sweet Master Campion." But of his academic career we know nothing. He had read the classical poets, that we do know, and wrote elegant Latin Verse—particularly hendecasyllabics. The volume of Latin Verse came out in 1595 ; an exceedingly rare book of which I have been unable to trace a copy,† but the collection was reissued, with additions, in 1619. We learn a little about Campion from these epigrams. In one place he tells us that he was " lean," and that he envied fat men ; he tells us, too, the names of a few of his friends. Some of them were Oxford men, belonging to Gloucester

as he has restored so much else that is good in Elizabethan literature, to a grateful and appreciative generation, to the occupation of a seat among the immortals, and to the permanent enjoyment of mankind."

* William Covell. " This work [Polimanteia, 1595] which generally bears only the initials W. C., has been attributed to William Clerke, but see Professor Dowden's letter in *The Athenæum* of July 14, 1906, p. 44." The Works of Nashe, ed. Mckerrow, Vol. V, p. 10, footnote 4.

† " In 1889 I had not been able to trace a copy. At a later date Mr. W. H. Allnutt informed me that a perfect copy (the only perfect copy known) is in the possession of Viscount Clifden, who has very kindly allowed me to make free use of this precious little volume." Note to the second edition of Bullen's Campion, February, 1903.

Hall, now Worcester College. There were the three brothers Edward, Thomas, and Laurence Michel-bourne, all of Gloucester Hall, with whom he was most intimately associated. They are known to have been poets, but published very little. Another Oxford friend was William Percy, a son of the Earl of Northumberland : he is known as the author of a collection of love-sonnets (of no particular merit), and he, too, was of Gloucester Hall.

There was yet another Oxford man, a poet, with whom Campion was very friendly, Charles Fitz-geoffrey of Exeter College, who took orders and got a living in Cornwall. With one Oxford poet, Barnabe Barnes, a lyrist of high ability, Campion for some reason or other quarrelled. A reconciliation was patched up between them in 1606, but they quar-relled again and Campion has many uncomplimentary epigrams on Barnabe.

But let us turn to the English Songs which are infinitely more valuable than the Latin Verses. In 1601 appeared the first collection, " A Book of Airs." The music was written partly by Campion, and partly by another noted composer—Philip Rosseter ; but all the poetry was Campion's. Some years before the publication of the " Book of Airs " Campion's poetry was known to a small circle of readers by being handed about in *MS.*, a common practice in those days. So early as 1593, in his " Honour of the Garter " George Peele had addressed Campion as

" thou
That richly clothest conceit in well-made words";

and in 1594 Campion had contributed a song to the Gray's Inn Masque " *Gesta Graiorum.*" This song was first printed in 1602, in Francis Davison's " Poetical Rhapsody," one of the very choicest of

our anthologies. It is a " Hymn in praise of Neptune,"
and runs thus :—

" Of Neptune's empire let us sing,
   At whose command the waves obey ;
   To whom the rivers tribute pay,
   Down the high mountains sliding :
   To whom the scaly nation yields
   Homage for the crystal fields
       Wherein they dwell :
   And every sea-god pays a gem
   Yearly out of his wat'ry cell
   To deck great Neptune's diadem.

" The Tritons dancing in a ring
   Before his palace gates do make
   The water with their echoes quake,
   Like the great thunder sounding :
   The sea-nymphs chant their accents shrill,
   And the sirens, taught to kill
       With their sweet voice,
   And ev'ry echoing rock reply
   Unto their gentle murmuring noise
   The praise of Neptune's empery."

From a dedicatory epistle by Philip Rosseter to
Sir Thomas Monson we are confirmed in the view
that Campion's songs had been circulated in MS.
Rosseter further tells us that the best of the songs
had been much corrupted in the course of tran-
scription, and that some impudent persons had coolly
laid claim both to the music and words of some of
the pieces. In this first collection of 1601 the songs
are full of beauty. Not the least beautiful is the
opening poem, which was suggested by Catullus'
famous lines " *Vivamus, mea Lesbia, atque amemus.*"

" My sweetest Lesbia, let us live and love ;
 And though the sager sort our deeds reprove,
 Let us not weigh them : heaven's great lamps do
     dive
 Into their west, and straight again revive :
 But soon as once set is our little light,
 Then must we sleep one ever-during night.

" If all would lead their lives in love like me,
 Then bloody swords and armour should not be ;
 No drum nor trumpet peaceful sleeps should move,
 Unless alarm came from the camp of love :
 But fools do live, and waste their little light,
 And seek with pain their ever-during night.

" When timely death my life and fortune ends,
 Let not my hearse be vext with mourning friends ;
 But let all lovers, rich in triumph, come
 And with sweet pastimes grace my happy tomb :
 And, Lesbia, close up thou my little light,
 And crown with love my ever-during night."

Here is another song in a different strain : it has
been sometimes attributed, without any authority
to Lord Bacon :—

" The man of life upright
     Whose guiltless heart is free
 From all dishonest deeds,
     Or thought of vanity :

" The man whose silent days,
     In harmless joys are spent,
 Whom hopes cannot delude
     Nor sorrow discontent ;

" That man needs neither towers
　　Nor armour for defence,
　Nor secret vauts to fly
　　From thunder's violence ;

" He only can behold
　　With unaffrighted eyes
　The horrors of the deep,
　　And terrors of the skies.

" Thus, scorning all the cares
　　That fate or fortune brings,
　He makes the heaven his book,
　　His wisdom heavenly things ;

" Good thoughts his only friends,
　　His wealth a well-spent age,
　The earth his sober inn
　　And quiet pilgrimage."

Campion was very successful in his sacred lyrics ;
Our poets as a rule do themselves but scant justice
when they turn their hands to devotional verse ;
their genius seems to forsake them ; they either
drop into commonplace, or are stiff and awkward.
It is astonishing, when one comes to think of it,
how very little devotional lyric poetry of high merit
we possess, how rarely do we meet the lyric cry
joined to religious exaltation. In Henry Vaughan
we find it, and we find it in Campion ; but I hardly
know another instance in English literature. George
Herbert is on a lower level, on a far lower level still
—far, far, below Herbert and infinitely below
Vaughan and Campion—stands Keble. There is
a fervent earnestness in Campion's sacred lyrics that
would startle the dullest hearer. You may search
your sacred anthologies without finding a mention

of Campion's name ; but I know not where you will find so clear a note, so impressive a summons, as in these lines :—

" Awake, awake thou heavy sprite,
　　That sleep'st the deadly sleep of sin !
Rise now and walk the ways of light !
　　'Tis not too late yet to begin.
Seek heaven early, seek it late :
True Faith still finds an open gate.

" Get up, get up, thou leaden man !
　　Thy track to endless joy or pain
Yields but the model of a span ;
　　Yet burns out thy life's lamp in vain !
One minute bounds thy bane or bliss :
Then watch and labour, while time is ! "

The next poem is written in a mood of quiet meditation and pious gratitude :—

" Lo, when back mine eye,
　　Pilgrim-like, I cast,
What fearful ways I spy,
Which, blinded, I securely passed !

" But now heaven hath drawn
　　From my brows that night ;
As when the day doth dawn
So clears my long imprisoned sight.

" Straight the caves of hell,
　　Dressed with flowers I see :
Wherein false pleasures dwell,
That, winning most, most deadly be.

" Throngs of masked fiends,
　　Winged like angels, fly :
Even in the gates of friends
In fair disguise black dangers lie.

" Straight to heaven I raised
    My restored sight,
And with loud voice I praised.
The Lord of ever-during light.

" And since I had strayed
    From His ways so wide,
His grace I humbly prayed
Henceforth to be my guard and guide."

I expect that Campion clung to the older faith.
Some of his intimate friends were Roman Catholics,
and he may have been related to Edmund Campion
the Jesuit, who was executed in 1581. But in those
days a wise man kept his creed (as far as possible) to
himself, and there is nothing in any of his writings
that could be construed into disloyalty ; he joined
in the general exultation over the defeat of the
Armada, and was whole-hearted in his outcry against
the Gunpowder Plot.

But for the most part Campion's songs are on the
subject of love, love in all its moods of high triumph
and dull despondency ; and in this love poetry of
his there is always a note of sincerity ; both his
sorrow and his joy are unfeigned ; there is nothing
frigid or conventional about him. He kept himself
tolerably free from conceits ; he wrote no sonnets
to his mistress' eyebrow, or to the pearliness of her
teeth, or the pink perfection of her finger-nails.
His diction is singularly clear and graceful : we
need never turn to a glossary to get at his meaning,
and though nearly three centuries have passed since
his songs were written, they are as fresh as if they
had been penned but yesterday. In one of his
prefaces Campion tells us " In these English airs I
have chiefly aimed to couple my words and notes
lovingly together." And he succeeded, for seldom

have verse and music been more happily mated. Occasionally the matter of the songs is thin and the wording careless ; but the music always rings true, our ear is never shocked by a jarring note, and when criticism has said its last word by way of disparagement, what a wealth of golden poetry is left ! More fortunate than Lodge or Breton (who could never wholly shake themselves free from the lumbering versification on which their youth was bred) Campion came at just the right moment. A singer when song-birds were many, his voice rose clear in all that musical medley, and can still charm us to-day, as it charmed the more delicate ear of the Elizabethans. Let us read one or two of the poems from this first collection :—

" Follow your saint, follow with accents sweet !
  Haste you, sad notes, fall at her flying feet !
  There, wrapped in cloud of sorrow, pity move,
  And tell the ravisher of my soul I perish for her
     love :
  But if she scorns my never-ceasing pain,
  Then burst with sighing in her sight and ne'er
     return again !

" All that I sung still to her praise did tend ;
  Still she was first ; still she my songs did end :
  Yet she my love and music both doth fly,
  The music that her Echo is and beauty's sympathy.
  Then let my notes pursue her scornful flight !
  It shall suffice that they were breathed and died
     for her delight."

And here is another ; a lover's plea that is old as Time.

" Thou art not fair, for all thy red and white,
 For all those rosy ornaments in thee ;
 Thou art not sweet, though made of mere delight
 Nor fair nor sweet, unless thou pity me.
 I will not soothe thy fancies : thou shalt prove
 That beauty is no beauty without love.

" Yet love not me, nor seek thou to allure
 My thoughts with beauty, were it more divine :
 Thy smiles and kisses I cannot endure,
 I'll not be wrapt up in those arms of thine :
 Now show it, if thou be a woman right,—
 Embrace, and kiss, and love me, in despite ! "

This last poem has often been wrongly ascribed to
Dr. Donne and also to Joshua Sylvester ; Sylvester
was quite incapable of writing it. If we want further
proof that it belongs to Campion we have it in the
fact that an early MS. copy, differing somewhat from
the printed copy, is preserved in one of the Harleian
MSS. in the British Museum—an MS. dated 1596—
and that it is there attributed to Campion.

In 1602, the year after the publication of his first
collection of songs, Campion published a prose
treatise, "Observations in the Art of English Poesy."
That Campion, a consummate master of rhyme,
should have written a treatise to prove that the use
of rhyme ought to be forthwith abandoned, is
certainly curious. In the dedication to Thomas
Sackville, Lord Buckhurst, author of the famous
Induction to the "Mirror for Magistrates," he
declares that the "Vulgar and unartificial custom
of rhyming hath deterred many excellent wits from
the exercise of English poesy." He then proceeds
to draw up a set of rules for writing English verse
on classical models, and illustrates his rules by
examples. Here is a short specimen of his unrhymed
verse, written in imitation of Anacreon :—

"Follow, follow,
  Though with mischief
Armed, like whirlwind
Now she flies thee ;
Time can conquer
Love's unkindness ;
Love can alter
Time's disgraces :
Till death faint not
Then, but follow.
Could I catch that
Nimble Traitor
Scornful Laura,
Swift-foot Laura,
Soon then would I
Seek avengement.
What's th' avengement ?
Ev'n submissively
Prostrate then to
Beg for mercy."

Those verses are smoothly written but how monotonous they would soon become! It would have been a sad loss to our literature if Campion had abandoned rhyme, but luckily he contented himself with issuing this odd little treatise. Metrical experiments were then in the air ; Spenser, you will remember, coquetted for a while with the English hexameter and placed himself under the tuition of the pedantic Gabriel Harvey. Campion's " Observations " seem to have made some little stir, for Samuel Daniel hastened to reply to them in his admirable " Defence of Rhyme." Daniel could not but express surprise that an assault on rhyme should have been made by one " whose commendable rhymes, albeit now an enemy to rhyme, have given heretofore to the world the best notice of his worth." We are grateful to Daniel for testifying to the fact that Campion was " a man of fair parts and good reputation." Ben Jonson wrote a " Discourse of Poesy both against Campion and Daniel," or so he told Drummond of Hawthornden ; if he did, it was never published.

Campion's next appearance was as a masque-writer. In 1607 he composed a masque for the marriage of Sir James Hay. Six years afterwards he wrote another masque, that was presented before the Queen at Caversham House near Reading, the seat of Sir William Knollys, afterwards Earl of Banbury. He also prepared in 1613 an entertainment on the occasion of the marriage of the princess Elizabeth ; and in 1614 he provided a masque for the ill-omened marriage of Robert Carr, Earl of Somerset, and Lady Frances Howard the divorced wife of the Earl of Essex. All these masques are constructed with much ingenuity (although Chamberlain speaks sneeringly of some of them in his letters) and the songs are often of a rare beauty. For some of them Inigo Jones arranged the scenery, and Campion gratefully acknowledged the obligation under which he lay to that admirable artist. On the other hand Ben Jonson thought that in the management of masques Inigo Jones used to take too much upon himself, and assailed him with bitter invective. But Campion was a man of more modesty than Ben. He saw that very much depended on the scenery, and he knew that unless the poet's efforts were seconded by the stage-manager the entertainment would fall flat. At the end of one of his masques Campion has a delightful address to the reader.

> " Neither buskin now, nor bays
> Challenge I : a Lady's praise
> Shall content my proudest hope.
> Their applause was all my scope ;

And to their shrines properly
Revels dedicated be :
Whose soft ears none ought to pierce
But with smooth and gentle verse.
Let the tragic poem swell,
Raising raging fiends from hell ;
And let epic dactyls range
Swelling seas and countries strange
Little room small things contains ;
Easy praise quites easy pains.
Suffer them whose brows do sweat
To gain honour by the great :
It's enough if men me name
A retailer of such fame."

You will notice what fine metrical effects Campion is able to achieve with these short trochaics—

" And let epic dactyls range
Swelling seas and countries strange "—

that last line is as ample as an alexandrine.

In November 1612 Prince Henry died, and Campion was among those whose griefs found utterance in verse. He issued in 1613 a small collection of songs " The Songs of Mourning " ; the music was composed by John Coperario—he was plain John Cooper when he went out to Italy, but he came back with the high-sounding name of Coperario. The songs are addressed to the King, the Queen, Prince Charles, Princess Elizabeth, the Count Palatine (who had come to England to marry the princess, and whose marriage had been postponed owing to Prince Henry's death) to Great Britain and to the World. Preceding the songs is a well-written elegy on the Prince, from which I will quote a few lines :—

Dr. Thomas Campion

" What could the greatest artist, Nature, add
T' increase his graces ? divine form he had,
Striving in all his parts which should surpass :
And like a well-tuned chime his carriage was,
Full of celestial witchcraft, winning all
To admiration and love personal.
His lance appeared to the beholders' eyes,
When his fair hand advanced it to the skies,
Larger than truth for well could he it wield,
And make it promise honour in the field."

In these funeral songs Campion was necessarily
somewhat hampered by his subject. They do not
rank with his best work.

The precise date at which he published his second
song-book is unknown, but it must have been sometime after November 1612, for he alludes in one
of the songs to Prince Henry's death. This second
collection is divided into two parts : the first,
" Divine and Moral Songs " is dedicated to the Earl
of Cumberland ; the second, which Campion calls
" Light Conceits of Lovers," is dedicated to the
Earl's son. There is a dedicatory sonnet to the
father in which Campion says :—

" What patron could I choose, great Lord, but you ?
Grave words your years may challenge as their
own,
And every note of music is your due
Whose house the Muses' Palace I have known."

Among the Divine and Moral songs are some most
delightful verses telling of a contented countryman
and his good Joan. The praise of country-life is a
trite subject ; but this old pastoral lyric of Campion's
has a freshness and charm that can never grow stale:—

" Jack and Joan they think no ill,
　But loving live, and merry still ;
　Do their week-days' work, and pray
　Devoutly on the holy day :
　Skip and trip it on the green,
　And help to choose the Summer Queen ;
　Lash out, at a country feast,
　Their silver penny with the best.

" Well can they judge of nappy ale,
　And tell at large a winter tale ;
　Climb up to the apple loft,
　And turn the crabs till they be soft.
　Tib is all the father's joy,
　And little Tom the mother's boy.
　All their pleasure is Content ;
　And care, to pay their yearly rent.

" Joan can call by name her cows,
　And deck her window with green boughs ;
　She can wreathes and tuttyes make,
　And trim with plums a bridal cake.
　Jack knows what brings gain or loss ;
　And his long flail can stoutly toss ;
　Makes the hedge, which others break ;
　And ever thinks what he doth speak.

" Now, you courtly dames and knights,
　That study only strange delights ;
　Though you scorn the homespun grey,
　And revel in your rich array :
　Though your tongues dissemble deep,
　And can your heads from danger keep ;
　Yet, for all your pomp and train,
　Securer lives the silly swain."

The following verses, a prayer and warning to his

relentless mistress, may be taken as a sample of the amorous songs :—

" Harden now thy tired heart, with more than flinty
  rage !
Ne'er let her false tears henceforth thy constant
  grief assuage !
Once true happy days thou saw'st when she stood
  firm and kind,
Both as one then lived and held one ear, one tongue,
  one mind :
But now those bright hours be fled, and never may
  return ;
What then remains but her untruths to mourn ?

" Silly trait'ress, who shall now thy careless tresess
  place ?
Who thy pretty talk supply, whose ear thy music
  grace ?
Who shall thy bright eyes admire ? what lips
  triumph with thine ?
Day by day, who'll visit thee and say ' Th'art
  only mine ' ?
Such a time there was, God wot, but such shall
  never be :
Too oft, I fear, thou wilt remember me."

Many singers of modern times have made free of this last line ; " the poet Bunn " being, perhaps, the best known example.

The " Third and Fourth Book of Airs " were published about 1617. We arrive at the date of publication in this way : the third book was dedicated to Sir Thomas Monson, and the fourth book to his son John Monson. Now, in 1615, Sir Thomas Monson was examined in regard to the Overbury murder. Of that grim tragedy we may never know the whole truth, but there were reasons for supposing

that Monson was implicated in the murder, and a
warrant for his arrest was issued in October 1615.
During his confinement in the Tower, Campion was
granted permission to act as his medical attendant,
and it appears that Campion himself was examined.
He admitted that he had received £1400 from
Alderman Elwys, brother to Sir Gervase Elwys the
Keeper of the Tower (Sir Gervase was executed for
his share in the Overbury murder) and that the
money was for the use of Sir Thomas Monson; but
he protested that he had no notion for what con-
sideration it was paid. As evidence of a definite
character was not forthcoming, Monson was released
on bail in October 1616, and was finally pardoned—
not acquitted, but pardoned—in February 1617.
When his pardon was granted he complained bitterly
of the manner in which he had been treated, protesting his innocence and declaring that Coke had
pressed the charges against him from a spirit of
malice. Campion's song-book was published after
the pardon had been granted; for in the dedicatory
sonnet he congratulates his patron that

> " those clouds that lately over-cast
> Your fame and fortune are dispersed at last."

Turn wherever we will in this last song-book we
find poems of faultless perfection :—

> " Kind are her answers,
> But her performance keeps no day ;
>   Breaks time, as dancers
> From their own music when they stray.
>   All her free favours
>   And smooth words wing my hopes in vain.
> O did ever voice so sweet but only feign ?
>   Can true love yield such delay
>   Converting joy to pain ?

" Lost is our freedom,
When we submit to women so :
   Why do we need them
When, in their best they work us woe ?
   There is no wisdom
   Can alter ends, by Fate prefixt.
O why is the good of men with evil mixt ?
   Never were days yet called two
   But one night went betwixt."

Notice the delightful rhythm. Here is another :—

" Now winter nights enlarge
   The number of their hours ;
And clouds their storms discharge
   Upon the airy towers.
Let now the chimneys blaze
   And cups o'erflow with wine,
Let well-tuned words amaze
   With harmony divine !
Now yellow waxen lights
   Shall wait on honey love
While youthful revels, masques, and Courtly
     sights,
   Sleep's leaden spells remove.

" This time doth well dispense
   With lovers' long discourse ;
Much speech hath some defence,
   Though beauty no remorse.
All do not all things well :
   Some measures comely tread,
Some knotted riddles tell,
   Some poems smoothly read.
The summer hath his joys,
   And winter his delights ;
Though love and all his pleasures are but toys,
   They shorten tedious nights."

To spend such nights one would be content to live in a perpetual winter. Here is a beautiful song sung by some saucy tricksy siren :—

" If thou long'st so much to learn, sweet boy, what 'tis to love,
  Do but fix thy thoughts on me and thou shall quickly prove.
      Little suit, at first, shall win
      Way to thy abashed desire,
      But then I will hedge thee in
      Salamander-like with fire.

" With thee dance I will, and sing, and thy fond dalliance bear ;
  We the grovy hills will climb, and play the wantons there ;
      Otherwhiles we'll gather flowers,
      Lying dallying on the grass,
      And thus our delightful hours
      Full of waking dreams shall pass.

" When thy joys were thus at height, my love should turn from thee ;
  Old acquaintance then should grow as strange as strange might be ;
      Twenty rivals thou shouldst find,
      Breaking all their hearts for me,
      While to all I'll prove more kind
      And more forward than to thee.

" Thus, thy silly youth, enraged, would soon my love defy ;
  But alas, poor soul too late ! clipt wings can never fly.
      Those sweet hours which we had past,
      Called to mind, thy heart would burn ;
      And couldst thou fly ne'er so fast,
      They would make thee straight return."

Then comes a melodious serenade sung by a poor starved lover beneath his lady's window, in the " nipping " and the " eager air " of a cold winter's night.

> " Shall I come, sweet love, to thee
>   When the evening beams are set ?
> Shall I not excluded be ?
>   Will you find no feigned let ?
> Let me not, for pity, more,
> Tell the long hours at your door !

> " Who can tell what thief or foe,
>   In the covert of the night,
> For his prey will work my woe,
>   Or through wicked foul despite ?
> So may I die unredrest,
> Ere my long love be possest.

> " But to let such dangers pass,
>   Which a lover's thoughts disdain,
> 'Tis enough in such a place
>   To attend love's joys in vain.
> Do not mock me in thy bed,
> While these cold nights freeze me dead."

Propertius never wooed his Cynthia in such tuneful numbers.

The poem that follows is even more beautiful. There is a MS. copy of it, signed with Campion's name, dated 1596, yet it has been absurdly attributed to Joshua Sylvester :—

> " Thrice toss these oaken ashes in the air,
>   Thrice sit thou mute in this enchanted chair ;
> And thrice three times, tie up this true love's knot !
> And murmur soft ' She will, or she will not.'

" Go burn these poisonous weeds in yon blue fire,
These screech-owl's feathers and this prickling briar;
This cypress gathered at a dead man's grave ;
That all thy fears and cares, an end may have.

" Then come, you Fairies, dance with me a round !
Melt her hard heart with your melodious sound !
In vain are all the charms I can devise :
She hath an art to break them with her eyes."

Then take these tender verses on his sleeping mistress :—

" Sleep, angry beauty, sleep, and fear not me.
For who a sleeping lion dares provoke ?
It shall suffice me here to sit and see
Those lips shut up, that never kindly spoke.
What sight can more content a lover's mind
Than beauty seeming harmless, if not kind ?

" My words have charmed her, for secure she sleeps ;
Though guilty much of wrong done to my love ;
And in her slumber, see ! she, close-eyed, weeps !
Dreams often more than waking passions move.
Plead Sleep, my cause, and make her soft like thee,
That she in peace may wake and pity me."

As an example of his lighter work we might choose
the song that tells how Midas gained his ass's ears
for preferring Pan's music to Apollo's :—

" To his sweet lute Apollo sung the motions of the
spheres ;
The wondrous order of the stars, whose course
divides the years ;
And all the mysteries above :
But none of these could Midas move,
Which purchased him his ass's ears.

"Then Pan with his rude pipe began the country
    wealth t' advance,
To boast of cattle, flocks of sheep, and goats on
    hills that dance ;
      With much more of this churlish kind,
      That quite transported Midas' mind,
    And held him rapt as in a trance.

"This wrong the God of Music scorned from such a
    sottish judge,
And bent his angry bow at Pan, which made the
    piper trudge :
      Then Midas' head he so did trim
      That every age yet talks of him
    And Phœbus' right-revenged grudge."

The next song shall show how a pert maid repulses
a suitor who had paid his addresses in what the lady
thought to be an awkward fashion :—

"Think'st thou to seduce me then with words that
    have no meaning ?
Parrots so can learn to prate, our speech by pieces
    gleaning :
Nurses teach their children so about the time of
    weaning.

"Learn to speak first, then to woo : to wooing much
    pertaineth :
He that courts us, wanting art, soon falters when
    he feigneth,
Looks asquint on his discourse, and smiles, when
    he complaineth.

"Skilful anglers hide their hooks, fit baits for every
    season ;
But with crooked pins fish thou, as babes do, that
    want reason :
Gudgeons only can be caught with such poor
    tricks of treason.

" Ruth forgive me, if I erred, from human hearts
  compassion,
  When I laughed sometimes too much to see thy
  foolish fashion ;
  But, alas, who less could do that found so good
  occasion ! "

Before I finish my quotations I should like to look
back for a moment to the first collection, the song-
book of 1601, and read a couple of the songs. The
first is of such rich romantic beauty that I know not
where it can be paralleled outside Shakespeare's
sonnets :—

" When thou must home to shades of underground,
  And there arrived, a new admired guest,
  The beauteous spirits do engirt thee round,
  White Iope, blithe Helen, and the rest,
  To hear the stories of thy finished love
  From that smooth tongue whose music hell can
  move ;

" Then wilt thou speak of banqueting delights,
  Of masques and revels which sweet youth did make,
  Of tourneys and great challenges of knights,
  And all those triumphs for thy beauty's sake :
  When thou hast told these honours done to thee,
  Then tell, O tell, how thou didst murder me."

The next poem shall be the last that I quote, for I
must make an end somewhere. If we let it sink into
our minds we shall put away whatever pride and
vanity we possess. Σκηνὴ πᾶς ὁ βίος καὶ παίγνιον, says
an old poet in the Greek anthology—life is a stage-
play and a sport. Campion powerfully enforces
the moral :—

" Whether men do laugh or weep,
Whether they do wake or sleep,
Whether they die young or old,
Whether they feel heat or cold ;
There is, underneath the sun,
Nothing in true earnest done.

" All our pride is but a jest ;
None are worst, and none are best ;
Grief and joy, and hope and fear,
Play their pageants everywhere :
Vain opinion all doth sway,
And the world is but a play.

" Powers above in clouds do sit,
Mocking our poor apish wit ;
That so lamely, with such state,
Their high glory imitate :
No ill can be felt but pain,
And that happy men disdain."

The last song-book, as I have said, was published in
1617. Two years later Campion issued the revised
edition of his Latin Verses, with numerous additions.
He died in 1620. In the parish register of St.
Dunstan's-in-the-West, Fleet Street, under date
1st March 1620 is the entry, " Thomas Campion
Doctor of Physic was buried." There is no record
of his having married. His will was made on the day
of his death, leaving " all that he had vnto Mr.
Phillip Rossiter and wished that his estate had bin
farr more."

Campion's fame stood high in his own days ; but
his poetry was quickly forgotten, being hidden away
in music-books that nobody opened. Modern critics
are only now at last beginning to find out that such

a person existed.* You may search the popular anthologies, and you will not see Campion's name mentioned. He is not represented in Mr. Palgrave's " Golden Treasury " ; and not one among the band of scholars whom Mr. Humphry Ward gathered about him when he prepared his four volumes of extracts from the English Poets could find a word to say in Campion's praise. But unless I am strangely mistaken there are no songs in our language more graceful, happy, and unconstrained—with more melody and magic—than many that we find in Campion's song-books. His contemporary John Davies of Hereford paid him a well-deserved compliment, when he wrote :—

" Never did lyrics' more than happy strains,
    Strained out of art by Nature so with ease,
So purely hit the moods and various veins
    Of music and her hearers as do these."

The praise is absolutely just ; for what strikes one most in reading Campion is his sureness of touch and his variety. Whatever he essayed to do he did well : he always found the true inevitable words, whether for a love song or a hymn. He was at once a born singer and a consummate artist.

* It has been thought well to let this conclusion stand, as it was originally written in 1889. But by the publication of " Lyrics from the Elizabethan Song Books " in 1887, and his edition of Campion's Works in 1889, Bullen gave to his favourite Elizabethan song writer so widespread an audience, that to the second edition of the Campion (issued in the " Muses Library " in 1903) was prefixed this warning note : " In 1887 Campion's admirers were few indeed. By critics and by anthologists he had been persistently neglected. I pleaded that the time had come for him to take his rightful place among our English poets ; and the plea was so successful that he now runs the risk of becoming the object of uncritical adulation."

William Bullein

William Bullein

THE old writer about whom I am to talk to-night, William Bullein, is not mentioned in the ordinary histories of English Literature ; yet he is an attractive figure and his prose— crisp and racy when he is telling a merry story— rises to heights of impassioned eloquence when he is delivering a solemn homily. We know little about him beyond what he tells us himself, but the auto-biographical passages in his works are distinctly curious. He sprang from the isle of Ely (where so many Bullens were and are to be found) and was born in the early part of Henry the Eighth's reign. Probably he studied at Cambridge, though the authors of the *Athenæ Cantabrigienses* could find no definite information on the point. For a time he lived at or near Norwich ; then his zeal for knowledge, par-ticularly for natural science and medicine, led him to travel widely in Germany, to wander over England and to push his way into Scotland. He is supposed to have taken his medical degree abroad, but before adopting medicine as a profession, he had taken Holy Orders and in 1550 became rector of Blaxhall, Suffolk. He resigned the living before November, 1554 to practise as a physician at Durham. One of his Durham patients was Sir Thomas Hilton, Governor of Tynemouth Castle under Philip and Mary. Unfortunately Sir Thomas died of a malig-nant fever while under Bullein's care ; whereupon William Hilton, the brother, accused the good doctor of having murdered his patient. This in-famous charge he keenly resented, protesting that Sir Thomas had " died of a feuer (sent onely of

155

God) amonge his owne friendes ; finishyng his life
in the christen faith." But when after a stormy
voyage from Tynemouth (on which he suffered
shipwreck, and lost not only a part of his library but
also a valuable manuscript) Bullein came to London
in 1560, William Hilton contrived to have him
arraigned for murder before the Duke of Norfolk.
He was honourably acquitted, but nothing daunted
Hilton then hired some ruffians to assassinate him.
The plot happily failed, but Hilton succeeded in
having him arrested for debt and thrown into prison
where he was kept some considerable time, and where
he wrote some of his books. It is pleasant to know
that Sir Thomas Hilton's widow had no hand in
this persecution ; far from sharing William Hilton's
blood-thirsty feelings she admired Dr. Bullein so
much as to become his wife.

Another person against whom Bullein was very
indignant was a Durham patient by the name of
Bellasys—R. Bellasys. Discoursing of the virtues of
the daisy " bellis," Bullein takes occasion to tell the
reader how he cured one Bellasis " not onely from
a spice of the palsie but also from the quarten."
Instead of being grateful for such a service, Bellasis
" more unnatural than a viper sought divers ways
to have murthered me : taking parte against me
with my mortall enemies." It is all very mysterious :
we seem to be reading some old romance from which
a number of pages have been cut away, so that we
can only make a guess at the plot. Why a man who
devoted his whole life to doing good should have
been pursued with such vindictive hatred, it is hard
to understand (save on the cynical theory that most
men hate their benefactors), and it is hopeless to-day
to try and discover the truth about William Bullein's
" mortall enemies." We must be content to know
that his wife, Sir Thomas Hilton's widow, loved him

and believed in him, and that the doctor died peacefully in his bed on the 7th of January, 1575-6. He was buried two days later at St. Giles' Cripplegate, in the grave where his brother Richard, a divine, had been laid in 1563, and where John Fox the Martyrologist was to be buried in 1587; a Latin inscription over the tomb commemorating all three, and particularly emphasising the fact that the kind doctor did not confine his attention to rich patients but devoted his services without distinction to rich and poor alike.

"The Government of Health" (1558) is the title of one of Bullein's treatises, and another work is called "Bulleyn's Bulwarke of Defence against all Sickness, Soreness and Woundes that dooe daily assault Mankinde" (1562). The "Bulwarke" was written in his prison days, and in it he gives us many little personal touches, as when speaking of the salt made in England, he says he had a share in the salt-pans at "the Shiles" (Shields) by Tynemouth Castle. He tells us too of cures he had wrought (and mighty proud he was of them!) on a certain Sir Robert Alie, a knight famous in his day for his skill in fortifications, and on Lady Hilton; of witches he had known in Suffolk; and of the untoward voyage to London that had ended in his arraignment for the murder of Sir Thomas Hilton; small wonder that, smarting under the memory of his wrongs, the good doctor should declaim against his "mortall enemies." But the only book of Bullein's that I am going to talk about to-night is "A Dialogue bothe pleasaunte and pietifull, wherein is a goodly regimente against the feuer Pestilence with a consolacion and comfort against death. Newly corrected by Willyam Bulleyn, the autour thereof," 1564. Of this 1564 edition only a single copy is known, which is in the Britwell Collection, where are preserved so many of the rarest treasures of our early literature. The dedicatory epistle to " Maister Edward Barrette of Belhous of Essex, Esquier " is dated " This twelfe of March 1564 "—which would be 1564-5. Although the title-page says " Newly corrected " no earlier edition is known to exist, and it is quite possible that " Newly corrected " may be merely a publisher's flourish and that there was no earlier impression (though others may prefer to think that there was an earlier edition of which all traces have now been lost). The book was reissued with some alterations in 1573 and again in 1578, when " pietifull " on the title-page became " pitifull " and " Bulleyn," Bullein. Three hundred years and more passed before another edition appeared, under the auspices of the Early English Text Society, in 1888.

And now let us see how the book came to be written. We have all been taught in our youth how Mary Tudor grieving in the last sad days of her sad life over Calais, declared that if her body were opened the name of Calais would be found written on her heart. As Froude says, the story "is not particularly characteristic but having come somehow into existence there is no reason why it should not continue to be believed." Elizabeth, jealous for England's honour, was constantly demanding (at the beginning of her reign) the restoration of the town, but France would not entertain the proposal. So in an evil hour the exasperated Queen listened to the overtures of the Huguenot leader the Prince of Condé and threw a force of English soldiers into Havre. In October 1562, Sir Adrian Poynings sailed from Portsmouth to Havre with the first detachment of three thousand men ; the commander-in-chief was Lord Warwick, Leicester's elder brother. Misfortunes at once began for the English troops. Soon

Condé made peace with his adversaries and implored Elizabeth to withdraw the troops. She declined, accused him of perfidious dealing, and in the spring of the following year (1563) sent out more troops to strengthen the garrison. Doubtless there were good soldiers among these hastily enlisted forces, but there was no time to pick and choose; so gallows-birds of all kinds—cutpurses, horse stealers, highwaymen—were taken from prison and despatched to Havre. The musters of the garrison were brought up to six thousand fighting men and one thousand prisoners, and in addition there was the English fleet. Some small successes were gained by the English and the garrison's prospects were beginning to brighten when suddenly, in June, a mysterious illness broke out: nine men died on the 7th of June; three weeks later the death-rate was sixty a day. The dreaded plague, the fever pestilence, was in the town and the garrison was doomed.

Elizabeth was slow to realise the horrors of the situation, and more and more men were sent to fill the places of them that had fallen; you may read about it all in Froude, and very ghastly reading it is. At last on the 20th of July, when famine was making an end of the poor remnant that had survived the ravages of plague, the Queen sent Throgmorton to negotiate the surrender. On the 29th of July, Havre was given to France, and the English troops—all that were left of them—departed under arms. When Admiral Clinton who had been detained by contrary winds, was invited by the French Queen-Mother to dinner, he explained that he could not leave his men, and to Monsieur de Lignerolles who brought the invitation, he added " that the plague of deadly infection had done for them that which all the force of France could never have done." The survivors reached Portsmouth in August, 1563, when Elizabeth issued a proclamation under her own hand commending their gallantry and urging upon all gentlemen, and all persons holding office, civil or ecclesiastical, to minister to their necessities. There was no effectual system of quarantine; the poor men scattered to their homes and naturally plague soon began to make its appearance in England. In August the London death-rate rose from two hundred a week (at which it stood in July) to seven hundred, then to eight hundred, then to a thousand, then to two thousand, and so through the sickly autumn till the November rains brought relief. As usual the clergy attributed the visitation to supernatural causes, while the sagacious Secretary Cecil took practical measures to counteract the evils of overcrowding in lodging-houses.

Of course in one form or another, plague was no novelty in England; but this particular fever pestilence imported from Havre was of an exceptionally violent character. When Bullein wrote—and certainly when the Dialogue was published in the 1564-5 edition—the force of the epidemic (in London at least, though not in some parts of the country) would have been spent; but in after years there would be other plagues, and the book would have lasting interest and value. After the visitation of 1563, people who had lost friends and relations or had witnessed the sorrows of their stricken neighbours would be heavy-hearted, and just in the right mood to welcome a book that mixed cheerful discourse with grave moralising. Bullein's object in writing was fully as much to keep people's spirits up in plague-time, as to preach religion (remember he had held a cure of souls) and morality, to denounce abuses and to give practical rules of health, with particular prescriptions for the treatment of the fever pestilence.

The Dialogue, or rather series of dialogues, opens at a London citizen's house. A north country beggar from Redesdale in Northumberland is at the door, and his voice is heard :—

"God saue my gud Maister and Maistresse, the Barnes, and all this halie houshaude, and shilde you from all doolle and shem, and sende you comfort of all thynges that you waude have gud of, and God and our derē Leddie shilde and defende you from this Pest. Our father whiche art in heauen, hallowed be your name ; your kyngdome come, your willes bee dooen in yearth as it is in heauen, &c.

Ciuis

Me thinke I doe heare a good manerly Begger at the doore, and well brought vp. How reuerently he saieth his Pater noster ! he thous not God, but you hym. Gods blessyng on his harte ! I praie you, wife, giue the poore man somethyng to his dinner.

Vxor

Sir, I will heare hym saie the Lordes praier better before I giue hym any thing.

Ciuis

What a reconyng is this ! Dame, doe as I commaunde you ; he is poore ; we haue plentie ; he is verie poore and hongrie ; therefore dispatche hym a gods name, and let him go.

Vxor

Softe fire maketh swete Malte : he shall tary my leasure.

Mendicus

Maistresse, if you be angrie with the saiyng of my *Patar noster* in Englishe, I will saie it in Latine, and also my *Debrafundis*. But so God helpe me, I do not ken nene of them bethe what thei meane."

Bullein was a very uncompromising Protestant, and loses no occasion of girding at the Catholic party. Puzzled by the beggar's accent, the citizen's wife says " me thinke thou art a Scot by thy tongue," at which he is mightily indignant.

Mendicus

"Trowe me neuer mare then, gud deam. I had rather bee hangad in a withie or in a cowtaile, than be a rowfooted Scot, for thei are euer fare and fase ; I haue been a fellon sharpe manne on my handes in my yonge daies, and brought many of the Scottes to grounde in the Northe Marches, and gaue them many greisly woundes ; ne manne for manne durste abide my luke, I was so fell. Then the limmer Scottes hared me, burnt my guddes, and made deadlie feede on me and my barnes, that now I haue nethyng but this sarie bagge and this staffe, and the charitie of sike gud people as you are, gud Maistresse: Ause I haue many of my sirename here in the Citie that wade thinke ne shem on me, yea, honast handcraftie men."

The citizen then inquires how he got through the city gates ; and he explains that wherever he went he found people from his own part of the country, who helped him ; among them being the " Bedle of the Beggers " a Redesdale man born. Then the citizen tells him that he too, was born in the north, came to London " yonge and verie poore " and now was in good case to live among his neighbours. Presently he inquires what news the beggar had brought from the country. " Nene but aude maners, faire saiynges, fause hartes, and ne deuotion, God amende the market ! " is the answer. Everybody

was going into litigation over trifles; rents were
being raised all round, there was great dearth and
much poverty; covetous men and hypocrites were
having things their own way, and soon there would
be a very hell upon earth. That was all the news
except that people were crowding into the country
from London to escape the pestilence. " I met with
wagones, Cartes, & Horses full loden with yong
barnes, for fear of the blacke Pestilence, with their
boxes of Medicens and sweete perfumes. O God,
how fast did thei run by hundredes, and were afraied
of eche other for feare of smityng." The citizen
says that he has sent some of his children into the
country, but that he intended to stay in London
himself; and he prayed God to deliver the town
from the plague because if it continued it would
destroy not only a number of poor people, but
many wealthy and lusty merchants as well. This
prospect seems rather to please the beggar than
otherwise, whose comment runs, that the poor who
succumb to the plague will be removed from their
troubles to a better world, and that many covetous
usurers will be cut down, " whiche dooe neuer good
vntill thei come to the dishe "; the beggars will
flaunt it in dead men's cast coats, jackets, belts and
shoes : " we beggers recke nought of the carcas of
the dead body, but doe defie it." On hearing this
the citizen advises him to go to the gates of the rich
Antonius, who was evidently in a parlous state, for
two hours ago Dr. Tocrub had ridden up on his
mule to the house and gone in at the gate attended
by his apothecary Crispine and his little lackey, " a
proper yong applesquire."

The name Tocrub is not found in the 1564 edition,
where he is styled Antonius Capistranus. Tocrub
was evidently an anagrammatised form of Burcot,
a foreign physician settled in London, who is

mentioned by Gabriel Harvey and in Chettle's "Kind Heart's Dream," and whose name often turns up in the State Papers. Again and again I have intended to find out more about him, for he must have been an interesting man ; but I have been too busy with other matters—or too lazy—to follow up the subject. Bullein had the strongest dislike of this Burcot ; he looked upon him as a man of high ability, but wholly unscrupulous and atheistical—what he calls a *Nulla fidian*.

In the second scene Antonius lies a-dying, but has not given up hope and is determined to die hard. The doctor Tocrub knows the patient has no chance ; the patient affects to think that it is all a matter of money—that the doctor can pull him through if the fee is made high enough. After a brief examination the doctor announces " These are no verie good tokens. . . . But I wil doe the best for you that I can doe by arte." Then the patient appeals to the doctor's cupidity. " You shall wante no golde, for though I lacke health, yet I want no golde of euery coigne, and siluer also." His warehouses are stuffed with goods ; he has brokers working secretly and wittily in the city and factories at Antwerp ; he has lent out money at thirty and forty in the hundred ; he has acquired broad lands in the country. He would be very loth to die, for here he knows precisely how he stands " but when I am gone I doe not knowe what shall happen vnto me." The doctor is cynically sympathetic :—

" You doe speake like a wise man as euer I heard, and moste thynges that you haue taken in hand haue greate profite with you. Of my parte I would bee lothe to lose you, bothe for an vnfained loue that I doe beare vnto you for your wisedome, and also for your liberalitie and giftes giuen to me many a time. Lo, here is the Damaske goune yet in store. Here is also a Flagone chaine of the hundred angelles that you did giue me in your last greate Feuer."

Our old writers (Shakespeare included) could never resist joking on the subject of angels. The dying man pricks up his ears.

"Who is able to resist suche a multitude of angells ? I thinke fewe doctours of Phisicke. But rather then I would dye I wil let flie a thousande more ; for these are the Angelles that shall keepe mee."

The wily doctor approves.

"That is the waie, I assure you, to perfite health; for that cause the Phisician was ordeined, as it is written : Honour the Phisician with the honor that is due vnto hym because of necessitie, for the lord hath created hym; and hee shall receiue giftes of the kyng, yea, and of all men."

Antonius

"That is a good swete text for Phisicians ; but why doe you leaue out these wordes in the middes of the matter, which is, Of the most highest commeth learnyng ? And so I doe remember I heard our Curate reade in the Churche, as by chaunce I came in with a Sergeant to arest a debter of mine."

Then they fall to talking of scripture and religion, the Doctor confidently stating that he is neither Papist nor Protestant, but a *Nulla fidian* as are so many of his profession. The patient owns that he is much of the doctor's way of thinking, but meanwhile he would be glad if the apothecary would provide him with " some good thinges for the bodie."

The third colloquy is between the doctor and the apothecary. While the doctor and patient have been talking, the apothecary Crispine has been strolling about the garden which is full of sundry kinds of rare flowers and herbs, with a fountain in the middle and with groups of statuary. One group represented the nine Muses "with strange instrumentes of Musicke" sitting under Parnassus, and then there were groups of the famous poets, garlanded with laurel and roses, with golden pens in their hands writing verse. Homer, Hesiod, Ennius, were shown; Lucanus apparelled in purple sat there "very high, nere vnto the cloudes"; moral Gower was there with "pleasaunt pen in hande, commendyng honest loue without luste, and pleasure without pride." Skelton, with a "Frostie bitten face" was frowning. Chaucer sat in a chair of gold covered with roses, writing "Prose and Risme, accompanied with the Spirites of many kinges, knightes and faire Ladies." Lamenting Lidgate was lurking among the lilies "with a balde skons" and a "garland of Willowes about his pate," while on a bed of camomile under a cinnamon tree was stretched Bartlet—Alexander Barclay—"borne beyond the colde riuer of Twede," with sheep and piping shepherds round him. Near by, in a black chair of jet stone, sat an ancient knight in orange tawnie "as one forsaken," bearing upon his breast a white Lion "with a Croune of riche golde on his hedde"—Sir David Lindsay of the Mounte.

I have considerably condensed this very curious description, given by the apothecary to Tocrub, of the wonders of Antonius' garden. It is however worth reading in its entirety, for it bears a marked resemblance to Dekker's oft-quoted purple patch about the bay trees in "A Knight's Conjuring." When it is remembered that the "Dialogue" was first issued in 1564 and " A Knight's Conjuring " in 1607, there would seem some cause for a shrewd suspicion that, even if he had not helped himself to as much as he wanted from the old doctor's pleasant pages, Dekker had the passage well in mind when he wrote the additional chapter on the *fortunæ insulæ*. That he knew the book there can be but little doubt. Bullein had a famous admirer in the person of versatile, redoubtable Thomas Nashe (and Nashe was Dekker's friend), who, in his " Address to all Christian Readers " pre-fixed to " Have with you to Saffron Waldon " 1596, writes :— " Memorandum, *I frame my whole Booke in the nature of a Dialogue, much like* Bullen *and his Doctor* Tocrub." Nashe used the edition of 1573 or 1578, for the name Tocrub does not appear in the edition of 1564.

I do not wish to press this point too closely. Such borrowings were not unknown then as now, and though at times hotly resented, for the most part were passed over in silence. Bullein died in 1575, three years before the third edition of the " Dialogue " was published ; the book was an old one, and who would trouble about a dead man's rights ? But if Defoe owed something to Dekker's " Wonderfull Yeare " (1603) with its moving account of the plague, did not Dekker himself (and for that very book) owe something to Bullein ? Now we will go back to the Dialogue.

Crispine would have run on telling more of the wonders of Antonius' garden (that he did not, more's the pity !) if Tocrub had not stopped him with " I will heare the rest of the matter at leasure," and told him to get on with his dispensing. " I haue spent all my fine Myrrhe," says Crispine ; and the doctor hints that inferior ingredients can easily be substituted. It was a charge constantly brought against apothecaries that they adulterated their drugs.

Stubbes in the "Anatomy of Abuses" touches on the subject, and Gabriel Harvey ironically remarks "There is deceit in all occupations but Apothecaries." Two rogues, Avarus and Ambodexter, are now seen approaching; they have heard that Antonius is at death's door, and have come to see whether they can trick the dying man into making them his executors or contrive some means of robbing him. The doctor goes off quickly followed by the apothecary, and in the fourth colloquy, Avarus and Ambodexter, discuss their nefarious plans. In the fifth scene or colloquy the doctor and apothecary go to attend the sick man, who tells them of the horrible dreams that have troubled him.

" Me thought I was in the top of a high Tower, telling of money, and sodainly there came an yearthquake and shooke the Tower in peeces, and caste mee downe vpon weapons all bloudie, whiche a great nomber of Morians had in their handes; from them I fell in the fire, which was like high mountaines aboute mee, whereas was muche noyse and a cruell battaile. I did see there many of myne olde acquaintaunce, whiche sometyme were of greate honour, both men Spirituall and Temporall, and the Pope hymself, with many of his frendes. They were in extreme wretchednesse, and sore handled of fearefull monsters, and wormes gnawyng vppon their breastes, vppon whom was written, Conscience hath accused me and hell deuoured me, *Ve, ve, ve!* And thus I am tossed to and fro. Alas, what shall I doe? Also I did heare many ragged and sicke people crie vengeaunce on me, and men in prison also, that said I had undoen them to inriche myself. Oh good God!"

The apothecary is conscience-stricken, and whispers

in the doctor's ear that he will go home and destroy the rotten drugs. " The vicar of S. Fooles be your ghostly father," says the doctor impatiently. " Are you so wise ? tary still with mee ; let hym paie for your rotten drugges, for I may saye to you that he is almoste rotten alreadie hymself ; me think your conscience is to much spiced with sodaine deuotion." Then he turns to his patient and assures him that his bad dreams are due to abundance of choler ; let him fear nothing ; whereupon the grateful patient hands him twenty " olde Angels " that have seen no sun for ten years, and also promises to reward the apothecary. Next comes in Wise, the surgeon, who bleeds Antonius. At this point the doctor learns that his mule has been stolen and flies into a fury, " I will hence ; I had rather lose xx. li. ; I will tary no longer."

Antonius expostulates. Leave him ! " What ! for xx. li. ? I will paie it double." So the doctor is content to stay, and then the dying man feeling his mortal body slipping from him, is fain to ask of this consummate hypocrite, " Is there a soule in man ? " " Yea, forsothe," says the doctor. " Why then," answers Antonius, " there must needes be a greater thing as the cause of euery liuyng soule, which I take to be God, which hath made all thynges ; and when you and I talked together you seemed that *Non est deus*." The doctor is surprised into frankness ; he holds the angels in his hand and knows that his patient is not likely to trouble him with many more questions. " I professed to followe *Aristotle*, but my meanyng was that I credite not the Bible matters ; I am no Diuine, I finde no reasons there for my tourne, they are to harde thynges for me." " Why," persists Antonius, " doeth *Aristotle* shewe any better reasons than is in the Bible ? Then I pray you what is the power of the soule ? "

There is in this scene between the doctor and his
patient a mixture of irony and pathos that over-
rides the author's determination to tell a racy story.
It is evident that he means us to pity Antonius, who
for bread is given the hard stone of philosophy ; for
though Tocrub was a doctor, but no divine, Bullein
himself was at home in either part. Having dealt
summarily with the soul, Tocrub discourses at great
length on the plague and the means of combating
it ; here he is on surer ground, and he cleverly con-
trives to keep Antonius' attention by holding out
hopes of his recovery. It is all very interesting, but
I must pass it over, as also the talk that follows
between the doctor and the apothecary in which a
number of prescriptions for the plague are set down
by the doctor, at the apothecary's request. The
apothecary (who throughout has shown more feeling
than the doctor) asks him if he will not be present
at the burial of Antonius, " if he dooe depart this
present worlde," to which the doctor replies :

> " He loued me as I loued hym, He me for
> healthe, and I hym for money ; And thei whiche
> are preseruers of the life of manne, ought not to
> be present at the death or buriall of the same man,
> therefore I haue taken my leaue, I warrante you,
> *Crispine ;* I will retourne to hym no more."

It seems that even the " angells " could not hold
him—poor Antonius !

In the next scene we go back to the citizen and
his wife. The daily ringing of the death-bells and
the sight of the ministers going their rounds to give
the communion to the dying and read the homily
of Death, then the grave-digging, the sparring in
of windows and the blazing of the blue cross—all
these things have got on the citizen's nerves, and he
is now ready to take his wife's counsel and go into

the country, though he is not without misgiving
that he may never return. Accompanied by their
serving man, Roger, a witty knave, they ride out
along the Barnet road. The citizen's wife is delighted
with everything she sees ; she has never been so far
as Barnet in her life, but it is Roger who is the life
and soul of the party ; he might well have ridden to
Canterbury by the side of the Wife of Bath, or
played the drawer with the Prince and Poins at the
Boar's Head Tavern in Eastcheap. At Barnet, Roger
tells how his grandfather " with twentie tall men
of the Parishe where I was borne " was sent to
fight at Palm Sunday battle in Edward the Fourth's
time, and how of all that " tall twentie " his grandfather was the only one that escaped. The night
before the battle he hid in the trunk of a " greate
hollowe Oke Tree with armes somewhat greene " ;
he was a thatcher, and climbed up partly "through
cunnyng," but "feare was worthe a Ladder to hym."
There in the hollow trunk this gallant soldier lay for
a month, living on acorns and nuts dropped by
squirrels, and for drink, catching the rainwater in
his helmet. " I neuer read this in the Chronicle "
observes the citizen. " There be many thinges "
retorts Roger, " (and it shall please your Maister-
ship), whiche are not written in the Chronicles, I
do think are as true as John your man doe read vnto
me when we doe go to bedde, almost euerie night.
I shall neuer forget them : fare wel, good Ihon ! "
" What are they, Roger ? " says the citizen, and then
Roger begins telling story after story with great
gusto. As a sample, I will read the story of Jack
Drake's medicine. It can hardly be an original story,
and I seem to have read it elsewhere—though where
I cannot recall. But how many stories are original ?
Original or not, it is uncommonly well told, and is
worth the hearing.

"Vpon a tyme when quacklyng Duckes did speake and caklyng hennes could talke, whiche indeede are continually companions bicause they are Foules (Marie of sundrie kyndes and names); for Duckes and all water foule doe not onely take the benefite of goodly pondes, riuers, and pleasaunte waters in the time of hotte Summer, with manie deintie meates, and at their pleasures they doe take the commodetie of the lande also. The lande birdes doe but onely liue vppon the lande as footemen; as for Haukes and fleyng birdes of the woodde whiche daielie persecuteth eche other, as murderers doe innocentes or cruell riche men the poore that would liue in reste, I medle not with them. Vpon a time the Drake with the duck and his neighbours, the Gese, beyng pleasauntlie disposed; as Iudas was, in plaiyng the traitour; onely to destroie the lande foules to the ende that they might enioye both land and water together at their pleasure. After the example of couetous men that would haue all thinges in their handes, and when one manne hath anie good profitable trade to liue vppon they will couette or vse the same, although their poore neighbours do perishe, and that is the cause of muche trouble, good maister, now adaies, that euerie callyng doe pinche and poule eche other, and where the hedge is lowest that commonlie is sonest cast to grounde, but the stronge stakes will stande in the storme. (I speake not of the lustie lawiers nor the mighty marchauntes; no, no, I will obserue nothing in them, let euerie Fatte stande vpon his owne bottome.) Nowe, saide the Drake to the lande fowles, good cosins, we are muche bounde vnto you for your daielie entertainement, good chere, and companie; we with our wiues and children are muche bounde vnto you; you are moste naturall vnto vs, we daielie feede and take of youre commoditie, come at our pleasures. Nowe, therefore, take part with vs, and vse your pleasure upon the Water; there is plentie of young Frie, and Fishe greate store, Sallet herbes of sonndrie kyndes, good against euery wound or grief, both meate and medicine, &c. Oh Lord, what pleasure is there to be had! come, sweete hartes, and let us take our progresse to the pleasaunt Riuer of Tagus, whereas the sandes of that flood are precious golde; there is both pleasure and riches; go and gather wealth and treasure; here is pouertie, there is sweetness, and here but stinkyng doung hilles; there is libertie, and here in bondage; there is ioye of the mynd, and here dailey feare of the Fox, that false Traitour. This sweet tale pleased well the lande fowles, as it is often tymes seen that faire woordes make fooles fain; notwithstandyng, the Cocke saide vnto the Drake: Gossippe, our bringyng vp hath been by lande, and our fathers also; we can not swim, wee haue no webbes in our feete to rowe withall as you have; we feare drownyng. What, saied the Drake, what nedeth these wordes emong frendes? Vse maketh perfitenesse; wee will teache you to swim by arte as well as we doe by nature (nothing is to hard to willing minds). Well, let vs go together; haue with you, saied the Cocke. Then, verie womanlie, the Duck did take the Henne by the hand, following their housebandes, whiche were arme and arme walking before; the Chickens and the Ducklynges followed in a goodlie traine, as it had been to a sumpteous Mariage betwene the Cockes eldest soonne with the pale face and the Drakes doughter with the pretie foote. At the water side the Drake with all the water foules did stoupe lowe and receiue their carriage, and when

they were all a cockehorse together they wente
into the water ; and eftsones, when the Drake
gaue his watche woorde, the water foules did all
sincke at ones, and all the land foules were sodainly
in a wrecke, and manie of them perished, and
some with muche a doe came to lande, as the
Cocke and the Henne, whiche returned home
with care and shame, and liued long in lamentation
and remained solitarie, without companie of
water foules. The Fox, whiche had games a both
sides, made the league with a learned oration
painted ful of Rhetorike, between them ; declaring
what unitie was between brethren and the fruictes
of peace, and so reconciled the water foules to
lande, where was a feined truce taken with muche
dissemblyng yet very good chere, shaking of handes
and kissyng, &c. Greate was the feaste at the
Cockes place ; the Nightyngale was there to
pleasure them with Musike, the Cuckowe songe
the plaine song soberly, muche daunsyng, and
after the same a costlie banket. As you knowe the
maner of the water foules dooe commonly sitte
nere the grounde, but land foules dooe mounte
vp to perche, and so they did. And when all were
at reste, secretly the cocke sent by the catte a
token to the Fox to come and doe execution emong
the ingratefull traitors. The cat was glad and ran
to the Foxe, findyng him in praier, and shortly
declared thambassage ; the Fox at the first re-
fused so hainous and bloodye a deede, declaryng
his indifferencie and righteousnesse, like a father
emong his children, and also what euill opinion
manie creatures causelesse had in hym. Marie,
saied he, I loue the cocke and his wife verie well ;
I also know how the water foules haue doen, I
haue made the vnitie betwene theim. I will
therefore not be seen in this matter my self, but

two of my sonnes shal do the feate ; goe you
before and clime in at the Windowe and open the
dore. So in fine it was dooen ; sodainlye the water
foules paied for the Malte grindyng, and were
slaine like flatryng ingratefull villaines. And this
is John Drakes medicen."

Another of Roger's tales, that of the Friar and
his boy (given in the 1564, but omitted in the later
editions) has some slight affinity to Browning's
Pietro of Abano in *Dramatic Idylls.*
When the citizen and his wife come to the inn
where they are to dine, Roger is all alert stirring
up the chamberlain and girding at the ostler :—
"You can make a stoned horse a geldyng, and a
longe taile a courtall. You knowe my meanyng well
enough ; hem, sirrha, I saie nothing but mum. I
haue seen you often in Smithfielde." The citizen's
wife bids him be quiet—"What, sir sauce ? you take
vppon you to plaie the Comptroller ? goe quietly
aboute your owne busines and let the ostler alone."
But Roger is irrepressible—"Maistres, it is merie
when knaues are mette. I did see him ones aske
blessyng to xii. Godfathers at ones" (a proverbial
expression that we have in the "Merchant of
Venice" and in Ben Jonson). While the meal is
preparing the citizen and his wife examine some
painted cloths that are hanging on the walls of the
"comely parlour" of the inn, and he explains to her
the meaning of the "writyng in those golden letters"
that she cannot read. When he has come to the end
of this rude picture gallery, Roger announces that
one Mendax—"in a greene Kendall coate, with
yellowe hose, a bearde of the same colour, onely upon
the upper lippe, a balde chin, a russet hatte, with a
greate plume of straunge feathers, and a braue
scarffe about his necke, in cutte buskens"—has

newly come into the inn, and is dancing trenchemore and telling stories about Terra Florida. The citizen sends Roger to invite the stranger to dinner. He promptly accepts, and when they are set at table at once starts telling most marvellous travellers' tales—such tales as one reads in Lucian's " True History," Sir John Mandeville's " Travayles " and the like. In the course of his perigrinations he had seen a unicorn thrust a dragon to the heart, the dragon retaliating by stinging the unicorn to death with his tail ; and to prove his *bona fides* he produced a piece of the unicorn's horn. Once when the soundings were being taken on a ship on which he was sailing, the sounding-board, new tallowed, came up with gold sticking to it. The captain sent down divers, and in three days thirty hogsheads of fine gold were gathered and two " buttes " of orient pearls. He had played at tables (back gammon) with the people called Fanesis, whose ears were as long as cloaks covering all their bodies. In parts of Ethiopia he had seen men transformed into lions and wolves, women into sows and apes by herbs of hot kinds ; and by moist herbs, men into fishes and women into apple trees ; but as no tale of wonder would be complete without a mention of King Solomon, so Mendax has seen " the chiefest citie " in that " exceedyng greate lande " Meroa, " sometyme Saba," where Solomon is tombed in all his glory. This tomb " nere hande as brode and as long as Westminster Haule " is made of pure crystal and gold, set with sapphires and diamonds, " xx pound waight euerie stone." Through this crystal, whoever had eaten of a certain magic herb, might see for the space of four hours in the night, King Solomon, Queen Saba and four hundred ladies " daunsing with noble graces in riche attyre, with garlandes of roses on their heddes " while round about the "inwarde border of the tombe" Seraphim played on lutes and harps. Then Solomon "as his daiely maner was" kissed the Queen and saluted her ladies, whereupon Cherubim, Seraphim and ladies vanished away, and Solomon "laie downe by the Queene vpon a riche bedde, and they twoo did sleepe there. Betwene whom there was a red hande holdyng a long naked Sworde, to guide the Queene, for feare of the thyng that you wot of" :—it would be worth a journey in Mendax' ship to the land Lekthyophages to search for this wonder-working herb.

But Mendax had not yet come to the bottom of his bag of tricks. He had been to the land of the Anthropophagi. The inquisitors of Spain had sent one hundred Friars into that land with orders that they should set up altars on their arrival, and "say masse in their holie golden clothes" which they did ; but when the cannibals "spied their bald pates and their coniuringes" they set upon them and eat them up. Mendax only escaped by eating a herb (given him by a witch) that transformed him into a dog, and he picked the Friar's bones. His boy was so strangely bewitched that he is a dog still ; and he shows the dog to prove the truth of the story. Again, in the land of Parthalia he found giants "tall men, sum one hundreth foote long, and verie olde" ; one of them, his interpreter informed him, was a labourer at Rome "when it was firste builded." And so on, and so on.

After dinner the citizen, his wife and Roger proceed on their way. As they ride along and Roger is explaining to his mistress that the lands thereabouts and some oxen she had particularly admired all belonged to her husband, he suddenly exclaims— "My maister hath risen so earely this mornyng that he noddeth as he rideth." "Sir," says the wife to the husband, "me thinkes I doe well perceiue you

totter as you ride. What ! are you asleepe ? Do
you not heare your mannes prating ? He is pleas-
antely disposed ; he would make me beleue that
you were a greate landed man, and had muche
cattell in store. Why, sir, how doe you that you
speake not to me ? " " Wife, wife ! God sende vs
good lucke : do you not see yonder cloude in the
Weste towardes the north commyng hether ? " In
the cloud appears a black lean long naked body with
no flesh on it, riding a pale miserable jade, and with
three darts in its left hand—one coal black, one
blood red, and the third dark pale. Thunder peals
and lightning flashes. " Kepe you close under that
cloke and stir not," says the citizen to his wife.
Roger takes to his heels, but the citizen knows that
for *him* there is no running away—no escape—from
Death. " If I doe runne, he is to swifte for me ; if
I tourne my backe, he will cowardlie kille me ; if I
dooe submitte my self to hym, he is mercilesse." The
thought occurs that he may bribe Death, who is
now beside him, with gold : he falls on his knees and
offers a bag containing one hundred pounds.

Singularly impressive are the speeches that Bullein
puts into the mouth of Death.

" You are well ouertaken, I am glad that wee
are mette together ; I haue seen you since you
were borne ; I haue threatened you in all your
sicknesse, but you did neuer see me nor remembred
me before this daie ; neither had I power to haue
taken you with me vntill nowe. For I haue
Commission to strike you with this blacke dart,
called the pestilence ; my maister hath so com-
maunded me ; and as for gold I take no thought
for it ; I loue it not. No treasure can keepe me
back the twinckelyng of an eye from you ; you
are my subiect, and I am your lorde. I will cut

of your iourney, and separate your mariage, but
not cut of your yeeres ; for thei are determined
when I should come : this is your appoincted tyme.
And when the tyme shal be appoincted me, I will
smite your wife, children and seruauntes ; thei
shall not bee hidden from me. I will finde them
forthe, be thei hidden neuer so secret, or flie neuer
so swift or farre of ; for I am so swifte that in a
moment of an eye I can compasse the whole
worlde, and am of so wonderful a nature, that I
can bee in sondrie places at once, and in sondrie
shapes. In flames of fire I often tymes doe consume
mankinde ; in the water I doe kill them ; I am
marueilous in woorke. I spare nothing that hath
life, but I bring all to an ende, & to mine own
nature, which is death."

The citizen pleads for time to " set his goodes in
order " for the use of his wife and children, but he
pleads in vain. Death tells him " I am the messenger
of God . . . and am the ende of life, whiche doe
separate the bodie from the soule. I am no feigned
thyng by the wise braines of the Philosophers " ;—
then Death hurls his dart. Roger, who has been
watching the strange scene, tells his mistress that
" the fearfull thyng that talked with my maister is
gone," and so the wife and the serving man go back
to the citizen.

" Sir," says Roger, " I am glad that he is gone ;
the deuill go with hym. Hath he taken all your
golde ? "

It is little the citizen cares now for his gold—"This
Death hath smitten me : I must dye." The wife
is for sending for " the best learned Phisicions in this
realme " ; Dr. Tocrub shall be summoned. The
citizen will have no doctor, but instead bids Roger
go with all speed and fetch Master Theologus " that

I maie haue his counsaile." To his distracted wife
he declares that he has put all his worldly affairs in
order ; that his debts will be paid, that poor men
who owe him anything are to be forgiven their debt,
and that restitution is to be speedily made to any
whom he may have wronged. There will be plenty
for her and for the children. Let her keep the com-
mandments of God as near as she can, and beware of
idleness and pride of heart : " Lament no more,
good wife, For who can kepe that must needes
awaie."

Roger soliloquises in a discontented mood—" I
haue spon a faire threde. I haue serued a good
maister with a mischeef ; he hath giuen me nothyng
in his will ; he is so spiritually mynded that he
forgetteth poore Roger, that hath taken paines for
hym thes ten yeres. Well, I haue had but small
gaines in seruyng hym, beyng an honest, faithfull
man." As he goes to fetch Theologus he resolves
what knauish course of life he will take up. If the
worst come to the worst he would turn tapster, for
of all potage he loves good ale. He anticipates that
his mistress will have a new husband within six
weeks, and " as the worlde goeth now adaies, she
will think it long ; out of sight out of mynde." His
final reflections as he reaches Theologus' house are—
" A Dogge hath but a daie. Let the deuill paie the
malt manne." Theologus goes to administer spiritual
comfort to the citizen (here we feel that Bullein is
speaking from past experience) who makes a good end.
Antonius had also sent for Theologus, but was dead
before he arrived, and Avarus and Ambodexter
were preparing a solemn funeral for him: with a
prayer for the passing of the stricken soul of the
citizen, the Dialogue ends.

I do not want to put Bullein's merits too high,
but I do claim that he is far superior to many

writers—old and new—that the caprice of present-day criticism has exalted. Doubtless he himself was free from literary vanity, but I, who bear his name and am of his kin, am jealous for his fame, and maintain here before the Elizabethan Society that he did enough to earn "a place i' th' story." When in 1888, the Early English Text Society published at my instance his Dialogue (to put it out of reach of oblivion), I promised to write a book of notes about him and give large extracts from his other works. My kinsman, Mark Bullen, was to join me; but alas! Death has hurled a dart at him—at him who cherished the old doctor's memory so fondly. Yet if quiet hours should come to me I hope to fulfil that early promise.*

Now I think I have said enough to show that Bullein was distinctly a man of parts, who could tell a merry tale with infinite jest, while in his graver utterances he may be compared—not to his discomfiture—with the acknowledged great masters of English prose.

---

* The quiet hours never came, and the notes are unwritten.

Hakewill's "Apologie"

Hakewill's "Apologie"

OF the many folios packed with curious learning that have come down from the seventeenth century not the least interesting is "An Apologie or Declaration of the Power and Providence of God in the Government of the World" by Dr. George Hakewill (1578-1649), sometime rector of Exeter College, Oxford, and its generous benefactor. His elder brother William was famous as a jurist and antiquary ; and in succeeding generations, down to our own times, members of this old Devonshire family of Hakewill have in various ways won distinction.

George Hakewill was a fairly voluminous writer, but his chief claim to remembrance rests on his "Apologie." In 1615 Bishop Goodman had published "The Fall of Man," wherein he laboured to show that Nature and Man are decaying. Hakewill took up the opposite position, and after long years of elaborate study issued in 1627 his weighty treatise ; a second edition, enlarged, appeared in 1630, and a third—again enlarged—in 1635. For the Cambridge "Commencement" of 1628 Hakewill's "Apologie" was chosen as the thesis for disputation, and Milton (then a student at Christ's) wrote a copy of Latin hexameters, "Naturam non pati senium," in support of Hakewill's contention. Samuel Pepys in 1667 read the "Apologie" and did satisfy himself "mighty fair that the world do not grow old at all" ; and in the next century, as we know from Boswell, it was one of Dr. Johnson's favourite books.

The treatise is dutifully dedicated "To my Venerable Mother the Famous and Flourishing

185

Universitie of Oxford," and the dedicatory epistle is followed by a preface in which Hakewill explains that the work was originally taken in hand for his own private satisfaction. Later, when he came to consider that his labours were for the vindication of God's glory and the advancement of learning, he resolved to make his book " publique for the publique good." He remarks pathetically, " While I have laboured to free the world from old age I feel it creeping upon myself."

Book I treats of " this pretended decay in generall." In the first section of the first chapter Hakewill deals with Divinity and contends that erroneous opinions thereupon were more common in former times than in his own day. There is much in this section, and in the four that follow, to remind us of Sir Thomas Browne's " Vulgar Errors " that appeared a few years after the " Apologie." Very curious are some of the examples that Hakewill gives of the far-fetched and fantastic opinions held on biblical subjects by old-time scholars. For instance, many had contended that our first parents spent but a single day in Paradise. Tostatus once held this view, but " upon better advice " recanted, doubtless coming to see—with another old scholar —that " so many and so different acts are by Moses recorded to have passed between their Creation and Ejection as could not well be despatched within the compass of one day." In the second section Hakewill touches on old errors " in philosophy." He denounces as an error the notion that the right hand is naturally more useful than the left, and urges that we should be trained to use both indifferently. Here he is in agreement with the Japanese of to-day and with certain American educational authorities ; and there can be no doubt that he is right. In commendation of the left hand

he writes, with a touch of delicate fancy, " if either
hand should in nature be preferred before the other,
methinks in reason it should be that which is nearest
the heart, the fountain of life and activity." The
third section is on errors in " History Ecclesiastical " ;
the fourth in " History Civil " ; the fifth in " History
Natural." He shows himself very sceptical on the
subject of the strange tales of credulous old natur-
alists. The long-lived phœnix he rejects ; he will
not allow that bears are licked into shape, that
swans sing before they die, that salamanders live in
the fire, or that hares are in one year male, in another
female. Most contemptuously he dismisses the old
notion that the sight of a wolf will strike a man
dumb ; nor will he be persuaded by Pliny that men
are sometimes turned into wolves.

The second chapter (in five sections) sets out the
reasons that induced the author to write and publish
his treatise. These were his desire to discover and
unfold the truth ; to vindicate the Creator's honour;
to show that the opposite opinion—the view that
nature and man are decaying—would " quail the
hopes and blunt the edge of virtuous endeavours,"
would make men careless as to their present fortunes
and the welfare of posterity ; and to point out how
weak is the ground on which this opposite opinion
has been based. Poets with their fables of the four
ages of the world impose on us ; and then we have
to listen to morose old men complaining of the
hardness of the present times and extolling the
past, the truth being that the change is in the old
men themselves, not in the world. There is such
a thing as an excessive admiration for antiquity—
" to prefer the wrinkles of antiquity before the
rarest beauty of present times."

The plan that he proposed was to treat of the subject first in general and then to come to particulars.

He begins by advancing six general arguments to show that the world is not decaying. One is that if a process of deterioration had been going on from age to age, the world would wear a changed aspect to-day : the warmth of the sun would have been impaired, cedars would have shrunk to the size of shrubs, horses would be no bigger than dogs, eagles than pigeons, pigeons than sparrows, and the whole race of men must have become pigmies. Having set out the general arguments against the pretended decay, he proceeds to state—and rebut —the general arguments for it.

In Book II, which treats of the " Pretended Decay of the Heavens and Elements and Elementary Bodies," Hakewill speaks wisely on the subject of astrology. He had read much and thought much, and—though he was what would be called an advanced thinker for his age—he did not at all share our modern lazy incredulity as regards the stars and their influence. (It may be parenthetically remarked that one of the master minds of the nineteenth century, the great Balzac, had a very poor opinion of people who deride astrology.) The early church, of course, had set its face against the astrologers ; and quite rightly, for Hakewill warns us very solemnly and very emphatically that the plain man had better leave astrology alone. He fetches his argument not from the Christian Fathers but from a pagan philosopher, Favorinus (quoted by Aulus Gellius), who weighs the prognostications of star-gazers thus :—

Either they pretend bad or good luck ; if good, and they deceive, thou wilt become miserable by a vaine expectation ; if bad and they lye, thou wilt be miserable by a vaine feare ; if they tell thee true, but unfortunate events, thou wilt bee miserable in minde before thou art by destinie ; if they promise fortunate successe, which shall indeed come to passe, these two inconveniences will follow thereupon, both expectation by hope will hold thee in suspence, and hope will deflowre and devoure the fruit of thy content.

In the matter of plagues, famines and earthquakes Hakewill maintains that we are less severely afflicted than in early times. In England leprosy had been stamped out before King James's days : the lazar houses, once crowded, stood empty or in ruins. As regards the complaints commonly heard that the earth is less fruitful than in former ages Hakewill quotes Columella, who wrote his books of Husbandry in the time of the Emperor Claudius. Farmers were then grumbling bitterly, but Columella denounced them as impious and told them it was their own bad farming that was to blame ; and Pliny the elder was of Columella's opinion. Hakewill was confident that the farmers of his own time were better off than they had ever been. There might be times of scarcity, but the horrible famines recorded by the English chroniclers were happily things of the past. If the earth had not lost its fruitfulness, neither had there been any deterioration in the beasts of the field, or in birds, or in fish, or in minerals.

In Book III Hakewill considers Mankind in regard to age, strength and stature, arts and wits. He concedes that the antediluvians and early patriarchs were granted prodigiously long lives and rejects the view that the years of Methuselah and the rest were spaces of thirty-six days—pointing out that such a system of reckoning would make Canaan and Enoch fathers at six and a half or seven years, and the patriarch Abraham seventeen and a half at his

death. On the Giants of Genesis he has much to
say and he estimates Ogg's height at twelve feet,
though others stretch him out to twenty-four.
After a display of much varied learning Hakewill
reaches the conclusion that in the course of the past
two or three thousand years there has been no
material change in regard to stature. " Our late
famous Queen Elizabeth " stood five feet nine, just
two inches taller than Augustus Cæsar.

Next he marshals his evidence to show that man's
bodily strength has not been impaired, and then
proceeds to consider the powers of the mind, arts
and sciences, learning and letters. His survey of
ancient and modern poetry is far from satisfactory.
He commends Chaucer and Spenser (though it is
doubtful whether he had more than a bowing
acquaintance with either), but he has not a word
to say about Shakespeare. Evidently he had little
taste for poetry save of the didactic order, but he
had been a deep student of divinity and had read
the Fathers with closest care : " I confess I rever-
ence their very names ; yet most certaine it is that
they all had their slips and blemishes in matters of
doctrine." Discussing architecture, he is enthusiastic about the beauty of English country-houses ;
of the colleges of the universities ; and of the town-
houses of the great merchants, particularly in
London. On the subject of navigation he is loud
in praise of Elizabethan seamen, particularly the
" noble-spirited Drake " ; and he wishes that some
learned pen would translate into Latin, for the
benefit of foreign nations, Hakluyt's " Voyages "
and Purchas's " Pilgrimes." Towards the end of
Book III he has an eloquent passage on the Mariner's
Compass, and an account of some obscure anticipa-
tions of a sort of wireless telegraphy.

In Book IV, which deals with the " Pretended

Decay in matter of Manners," Hakewill ransacks
the Fathers to depict in glowing colours the de-
pravities of the ancient world ; and, needless to say,
he is steeped in Tacitus, Suetonius, Dion Cassius,
Martial. In describing the luxury of imperial Rome
he tells us of Domitian's palace ; of Nero's golden
house, with its three galleries, each a mile long ;
and of those stately cedarn barges (with their sails
of many colours, and their sterns inlaid with pearls
and precious stones) in which Caligula sailed up and
down the coast of Campania.

The later part of the Fourth (and last) Book is
taken up with disquisitions on the end of the world,
the joys of heaven and the torments of hell ; but
into these mysteries we cannot, in the limits of the
present paper, follow him.

Fulke Greville, Lord Brooke

Fulke Greville, Lord Brooke

FULKE GREVILLE—member of an ancient and honourable Warwickshire family—was born ten years before Shakespeare and survived him by fourteen years. Without attempting to go far back into the records of Greville's family history we may note that his grandfather, also a Fulke Greville, was a distinguished soldier in the time of Henry VIII, and, dying in 1559, was buried in Alcester Church, where there is a fine monument to his memory. Fulke Greville the second, our poet's father, is described by Camden as " a man no less esteemed for the sweetness of his temper than the dignity of his station." He married Anne Neville, daughter of Ralph Neville, Earl of Westmorland ; and there were two children by the marriage—Fulke Greville, the poet and statesman who is the subject of this lecture, and Margaret, who married Sir Richard Verney, ancestor of the Lords Willoughby de Broke.

The poet was born at the family seat of the Grevilles, Beauchamp Court, in 1554, and in 1564 was sent to Shrewsbury School. Sir Philip Sidney entered the school on the same day ; he was of the same age as Greville, and his name stands just above Greville's in the school register. A warm friendship sprang up between the two boys ; and to the end of his long life Greville never ceased to cherish and honour the memory of this friend of his boyhood and early manhood—the famous soldier, courtier and poet, the best-beloved man of the Elizabethan age, whose untimely loss was passionately bewailed not only in England but throughout the protestant states of Europe. In old age Greville occupied himself with writing a memoir of his early friend ; and on his monument at St. Mary's Church at Warwick may still be read the inscription which Greville had cut for himself, recording that he had been " Servant to Queene Elizabeth, Counceller to King James, Frend to Sir Philip Sidney."

From Shrewsbury School Sidney went to Christ Church, Oxford, and Greville to Jesus College, Cambridge. Boys were sent to the universities earlier in those days than in these ; young Greville was only fourteen when he passed to Cambridge. Little or nothing is known of his Cambridge career. On leaving the university he was anxious to secure some active employment abroad, but the Queen would not allow him to see military service on the Continent. On one occasion he had actually obtained the royal permission to cross to the Low Countries and take part in the fighting ; but at the last moment —when all his preparations had been made and his horses were being shipped at Dover—the Queen changed her mind and sent down in hot haste a special messenger, Sir Edward Dyer, to forbid him to leave England. On another occasion, without asking the Queen's leave, young Greville stole abroad in the train of Secretary Walsingham ; but Elizabeth signified her displeasure by refusing—on his return—to admit him to her presence for many months. In 1558 Sidney and Greville contemplated going on an expedition against the Spanish West Indies with Sir Francis Drake. The young men had reached Plymouth and were preparing to embark, when the Queen peremptorily called them back and Drake had to start without them. When Lord Leicester went to the Low Countries as General of the Queen's forces—on the expedition in which Sidney lost his life—he offered Greville command of

a hundred horse, but again " this excellent lady "
(as he calls her—with, I think, a touch of asperity)
declined to let him go. Elizabeth was a born ruler,
and took care to let her proudest subjects know
she was a mistress who must be obeyed. But she
may have had very good reasons for withholding
her consent. Though Fulke Greville lived to old
age his health was never robust ; and the Queen
may well have thought that he was far better fitted
to fill civil appointments in England than to trail
a pike in the Low Countries. Like a prudent man,
Greville saw it would be unwise to oppose the
Queen's wishes ; so he called his second thoughts to
council ; and seeing that it was " sufficient for the
plant to grow where his Sovereign's hand had placed
it " he found reason to contract his thoughts " from
their larger but wandering horizon of the world
abroad " and to bound his prospects within the safe
limits of duty " in such home services as were
acceptable to my sovereigne." Occasionally he was
allowed to go abroad. In 1579 he accompanied
Sidney's friend Languet to Germany, and on his
way back had an interview with William the Silent.

For a time he held some small office under Sir
Henry Sidney (father of his friend Philip Sidney),
the Lord President of the Marches ; and afterwards
he was " Clerk of the Signet to the Council in
Wales." It is very difficult to realise precisely what
the duties and emoluments of minor offices were in
Elizabeth's reign. It is stated that as " Clerk of the
Signet " he drew a matter of £2,000 a year—which
would be equal to nearly £10,000 a year of our
money—but I should imagine that the emoluments
have been grossly exaggerated. If you will look into
the calendars of State Papers you will see that
officials are constantly complaining that their salaries
are all in arrears. Nowadays a civil servant gets his

cheque monthly or quarterly; but in Elizabeth's day a man had to get his money how he could. It is absurd to suppose that young Fulke Greville drew £10,000 a year (of present-day money) as "Clerk of the Signet," but no doubt he got what he could—and when he could—if there happened to be any money available. In that wonderful Elizabethan age everything is mysterious; and not the least mysterious point is how the civil servants at home—and particularly abroad—were paid their salaries; and what relation the actual sums paid bore to the nominal salaries. Some—unscrupulous—persons got a great deal for doing very little; and some who worked early and late, giving the best years of their life to the service of their country, were abominably ill-paid or were actually out of pocket.

In 1583 Greville was appointed secretary for the principality of Wales, and in 1603 was confirmed in this office for life. Seemingly he was able to discharge most of the duties by deputy; for certainly he did not take up his residence in Wales. In this same year—1583—he was in London, entertaining the famous Giordano Bruno. Four years later, when Sir Philip Sidney was buried in state in St. Paul's, Greville was one of the pall bearers. Sidney by his will left his books to Greville and Sir Edward Dyer.

For a short time in 1591 Greville served with the English forces in Normandy under Henry of Navarre. Three years later he was using his influence with Elizabeth on behalf of Francis Bacon, who was seeking the office of solicitor-general. His relations with Bacon seem to have been most friendly; but Arthur Wilson, a gossipy writer of the next century who related many scandalous anecdotes of the Court of King James, is the authority for a statement

which—if it were true—would be highly discreditable
to Greville's memory. The statement is this—that
when Bacon fell into disgrace and was living in
retirement in his chambers in Gray's Inn he found
that he could not relish the beer provided by the
inn and sent a messenger to beg a bottle of beer
from Greville, who ordered his butler to refuse the
ex-chancellor's very modest request. The story
seems absolutely incredible. We know that in 1621,
when James I sent to Greville the MS. of Bacon's
History of Henry VII to see whether—for state
reasons—any alterations were needed, Brooke returned the work to the King with high commenda-
tions. Bacon himself has left it on record that
Greville used his influence with Queen Elizabeth
" honourably and did many men good." We may,
I think, simply dismiss Wilson's anecdote as a piece
of idle, malicious gossip.

In 1598 Greville became—what was called—
Treasurer of the Wars, and later in the same year
Treasurer of the Navy. The Queen seems to have
lost no opportunity of putting promotion in his
way. Sir Robert Naunton (in " Fragmenta Regalia ")
goes so far as to say that Greville " had the longest
lease and the smoothest time without rub of any of
her favourites." Nor was his influence diminished
when James I came to the throne. In 1605 James
bestowed upon him Warwick Castle, which had
fallen into a ruinous state. Dugdale calculates that
Greville spent upwards of £20,000—about £100,000
of our money—in putting the castle into repair,
adorning it with rich furniture, and laying out the
gardens. In 1614 Greville succeeded Sir Julius
Cæsar as Chancellor and Under-Treasurer of the
Exchequer ; and in 1621 he was created Baron
Brooke, the title borne by his ancestors the Wil-
loughbies. Among the smaller offices that he held

was the recordership of Stratford-on-Avon, and there are many references to him in the Stratford records. His later years were passed in comparative seclusion. He died under the following somewhat mysterious circumstances. Being unmarried he had settled all his property on his cousin Robert Greville; and his will was witnessed by several gentlemen in his service, among them being one Ralph Heywood, a retainer of many years' standing. Some months after the making of his will he added a codicil giving bequests to these gentlemen but omitting Heywood's name. The old retainer expostulated with him and—in the altercation that ensued—stabbed him in the back with a dagger, afterwards cutting his own throat. This happened on the 1st September 1628, and Greville died of the wound at the end of the month. One might wish that he had met his death in some other way. An anonymous rhymester of the time hints that he received his due deserts by treating an old dependent shabbily; but the affair is a mystery to which we have no clue. Meanness was certainly not a trait in Greville's character. Many of his contemporaries bore ample testimony to his generosity—among them Samuel Daniel, the poet; John Speed, the annalist; Camden, the historian and antiquary—all three had enjoyed his patronage, as they gratefully acknowledged. Shakespeare's godson, Sir William Davenant, was in his youth befriended by Greville, who employed him as page—an employment that young gentlemen in those days were glad to accept. You will remember that a famous Warwickshire poet, Michael Drayton, served as page in his youth.

To turn now from Greville's life to his writings. With the exception of some small poems that appeared in Dowland's Song-books, "England's Helicon" and one or two other anthologies,—and the tragedy of " Mustapha," which was published in 1609—nothing of Greville's was issued during his lifetime ; but in 1633 were posthumously issued " Certaine Learned and elegant Workes of the Right Honourable Fulke, Lord Brooke, written in his Youth and Familiar Exercise with Sir Philip Sidney " ; these were followed in 1652 by the prose " Life of the Renowned Sir Philip Sidney," and in 1670 by the " Remains of Sir Fulk Grevill, Lord Brooke, being Poems of Monarchy and Religion."

The group of poems entitled " Cælica in CX Sonnets " doubtless contains his earliest verse. The greater part of them are love-poems in irregular metres—not sonnets in the strict sense—and are clearly written in imitation of Sir Philip Sidney ; but towards the end of the series are several pieces that are not at all of an amatory character. Greville's modern editor, the late Dr. Grosart, found his love-poetry full of intense passion, keen emotion, forceful utterance—and wrote rather ridiculously about it. As a matter of fact there is nothing to run into raptures about. Greville in his youth wrote love-poetry because everybody else was writing it ; a few of the poems are elegantly and playfully turned, but it is the shallowest nonsense to claim that these early and imitative love-verses enshrine the record of a great passion.

Greville was above everything else a thinker—a very deep and subtle thinker—and it is his meditative and philosophical poems—the ripe fruits of his study—that claim our attention ; not his youthful echoes from Sidney's Arcadia. Southey—than whom we have had few better critics—called Greville the most thoughtful of poets ; and Charles Lamb, a greater critic than Southey, remarked that in reading Greville " We shall find all frozen and made rigid with intellect. . . . It requires a study equivalent

to the learning of a new language." There are three
considerable poets of the Elizabethan and Jacobean
age whom it is exceedingly difficult for present-day
readers to follow. One is Fulke Greville, another is
George Chapman, and the third is John Donne ;
and perhaps the most difficult of the three is Fulke
Greville. Chapman was a professional man of letters ;
he was without means and had somehow to make a
living by his pen, no easy matter in those days : but
he had a great contempt for the public, and—in
spite of the stings of poverty—preserved his inde-
pendence as completely as Donne, who after early
struggles had been promoted to the Deanery of St.
Paul's, or as Lord Brooke, the owner of countless
broad acres, one of the wealthiest men of his generation. For literary fame, at least for the applause of
critics, Chapman, Greville and Donne cared nothing :
and what cared Shakespeare, greater—infinitely
greater—than all of them put together ? There is
a striking passage in Greville's Memoir of Sidney—
" For my own part I found my creeping Genius
more fixed upon the Images of Life than the Images
of Wit, and therefore chose not to write to them
on whose foot the black Oxe had not already trod,
as the Proverbe is, but to those only that are weather-
beaten in the Sea of this World, such as having lost
the sight of their Gardens and Groves study to
saile on a right course among Rocks and quicksands."
This is an eloquent way of saying that he was more
intent upon the matter than the form. Judged as a
whole his work must be allowed harsh and untunable,
deliberately harsh. That he might have written
smoothly, had he so chosen, some of his earlier
poems amply testify. As a fair example of his early
work I will quote the following :—

Fulke Greville, Lord Brooke

" Away with these self-loving lads,
    Whom Cupid's arrow never glads :
    Away poor souls, that sigh and weep,
    In love of those that lie asleep :
        For Cupid is a meadow god
        And forceth none to kiss the rod.

" Sweet Cupid's shafts like Destiny
    Do causeless good or ill decree ;
    Desert is borne out of his bow,
    Reward upon his wings doth go :
        What fools are they that have not known
        That Love likes no laws but his own.

" My songs they be of Cynthia's praise,
    I wear her rings on holidays ;
    In every tree I write her name
    And every day I read the same :
        Where Honour Cupid's rival is
        There miracles are seen of his.

" If Cynthia crave her ring of me
    I blot her name out of the tree ;
    If doubt do darken things held dear
    Then well-fare nothing once a year :
        For many run, but one must win,
        Fools only hedge the cuckoo in.

" The worth that worthiness should move
    Is love, that is the bow of love :
    And love as well the shepherd can
    As can the mighty noble-man :
        Sweet Saint, 'tis true you worthy be,
        Yet without love nought worth to me."

Those verses were set to music by John Dowland,
the lutenist, in 1597, and trip gracefully enough.

Now I will quote a passage to show him in his later and graver vein. I select the opening stanzas of his "Treatise of Human Learning" :—

" The Mind of Man is this world's true dimension,
   And Knowledge is the measure of the mind :
   And as the mind, in her vast comprehension,
   Contains more worlds than all the world can find,
       So knowledge doth it selfe farre more extend
       Than all the minds of men can comprehend.

" A climbing height it is without a head,
   Depth without bottom, way without an end ;
   A circle with no line invironed ;
   Not comprehended, all it comprehends ;
       Worth infinite, yet satisfies no minde
       Till it that infinite of the Godhead find.

" This Kowledge is the same forbidden tree
   Which man lusts after to be made his Maker ;
   For Knowledge is of Power's eternity,
   And perfect Glory, the true image-taker ;
       So as what doth the Infinite containe,
       Must be as infinite as it again."

Here, though the thought is weighty and close-packed, the language is not difficult ; but frequently both sense and language are veiled in obscurity.

It needs a good deal of resolution to read Greville's works continuously for many pages together ; but if we persevere we are rewarded by coming across memorable thoughts and images. Here is a solemn passage from one of his later sonnets :—

" But when this life is from the body fled
   To see itself in that eternall glasse
   Where Time doth end, and thoughts accuse the
       dead,

Fulke Greville, Lord Brooke

Where all to come is one with all that was ;
Then living men aske how he left his breath
That while he lived never thought of death."

Not seldom single lines start out from their sur-
roundings and impress themselves vividly on the
memory, as thus :—

"Life is a top which Whipping Sorrow driveth"

or this from the "Treatise of Warres"—

"Nor by the Warres doth God revenge alone
He sometimes tries and travelleth the good ;
Sometimes again to have His honor known,"

now comes the fine line—

"He makes corne growe where Troy itselfe once
stood."

Here is a telling line—

"Impossible is but the faith of fear."

and then another—

"Contempt deposeth Kings as well as death."

Greville had not a spark of dramatic genius, but
he threw two of his works, "Mustapha" and
"Alaham," into the form of plays. He is careful to
tell us that they were not "plaies for the stage."
They are in the nature of moral and political treatises,
the author's design being, in his own words, "to
trace out the high waies of ambitious Governors and
to show in the practice that the more audacity,
advantage and good success such Soveraignties have,
the more they hasten to their own desolate and
ruine." Like Samuel Daniel, Sir William Alexander,
and one or two other writers of that age, he took

the frigid rhetorical tragedies of Seneca as his model. But some of his most pregnant utterances are to be found in the choruses of these Senecan plays. In practical state affairs Greville was a strong upholder of the King's prerogative, but in his speculative opinions he shows a good deal of sympathy with republicanism. His views, too, on church matters were of a liberal character. In reading him we come to regard him rather as a lofty-minded puritan and republican than as a Church-and-King man. But it is difficult to classify him, and so we had better be satisfied with the description that Robert Southey gave of him—that he is the most thoughtful of poets.

Shakespeare, the Englishman

Shakespeare, the Englishman

THE spirit of patriotism burned brightly in Elizabethan England, and the poets of that age were always happily inspired when they were singing England's praises or hurling defiance at her foes. In 1593 was published a poor chronicle play, "Edward I," written by George Peele, who was born six years before Shakespeare. It is a hasty, unsatisfactory, and in some respects repulsive piece of journeyman work, quite the worst of Peele's writings ; yet, at one point, stirred by a vision of England's greatness, his fumbling Muse suddenly passes from riffraff rodomontade to clear, dignified, poetic utterance :

" Illustrious England, ancient seat of Kings,
  Whose chivalry hath royalised thy fame,
  That, sounding bravely through terrestrial vale,
  Proclaiming conquests, spoils, and victories,
  Rings glorious echoes through the furthest world ;
  What warlike nation, trained in feats of arms,
  What barbarous people, stubborn or untamed,
  What climate under the meridan signs,
  Or frozen zone under his brumal plage [shore],
  Erst have not quaked and trembled at the name
  Of Britain and her mighty Conquerors ? "

Not a few of the Elizabethan poets had seen service on land or sea. The heroic Sir Philip Sidney was the beau-ideal of a soldier-poet ; but that dreamer of opulent dreams, the poets' poet, Edmund Spenser, who reveals to us in the " Faerie Queen " a fantastic wonder-world of romantic beauty, had a practical knowledge of the art of war, as was expressly stated by Queen Elizabeth when she appointed him in 1598 Sheriff of Cork, " being a man endowed with good knowledge in learning, and not unskilful or without experience in the wars." Famous, ill-starred Sir Walter Raleigh, courtier, soldier, mariner, empire-builder, not only wrote excellent prose, but in the few (too few) examples that have been preserved of his verse shows himself to be a poet of rare quality. Shakespeare's friend and panegyrist, Ben Jonson, fought in his younger days in the Low Countries, and on his memorable visit to William Drummond, the Laird of Haw-thornden, related how he had challenged and killed one of the enemy in single combat in the view of both armies. Probably he took greater pride in this achievement than in his masterly comedy " Volpone " or his solidly-built tragedy " Sejanus," though no poet regarded his own writings with more complacency than arrogant, free-hearted, adored, maligned Ben Jonson.

Thomas Lodge's pastoral romance " Rosalynde," to which Shakespeare was indebted in " As You Like It," was written at sea off the Canaries when the author was serving in an expedition against the Spaniards. Among professional soldiers who engaged in authorship may be mentioned the voluminous and versatile George Gascoigne, whose satire, " The Steel Glass," is one of the earliest specimens of English blank verse ; Thomas Churchyard, whose " Legend of Jane Shore " was extravagantly praised in its day ; Barnabe Rich, a pioneer romance-writer from whom Shakespeare borrowed the plot of " Twelfth Night " ; and George Whetstone, whose play of " Promos and Cassandra " (1578) supplied more than a hint for " Measure for Measure."

Of Shakespeare's early manhood we know nothing. At eighteen he married a woman of six-and-twenty, who bore him within two years a daughter and twins (boy and girl). As his father, who had probably never been enthusiastic over the early marriage, was about this time financially embarrassed, the young Shakespeare would naturally decide to leave Stratford-on-Avon and seek his fortunes in the world. But where he went and what he did before he took to the stage will probably never be ascertained. Lord Chancellor Campbell was so struck with the legal knowledge displayed by Shakespeare that he wrote a book to show the poet must have had a professional training in the law. W. J. Thoms, the founder of "Notes and Queries," was convinced that Shakespeare served as a soldier under Leicester in the Low Countries. Others suggest that he may have been employed in the London printing-office of Vautrollier, to whom another Stratford-on-Avon boy (who was to print "Venus and Adonis" and "Lucrece") had been apprenticed; and some favour the theory that he had been a schoolmaster. It is a case of "believe as you list," for—unless some documentary evidence should chance hereafter to be discovered—the mystery will remain impenetrable. One of the master-spirits of the nineteenth century was the great French novelist, Honoré de Balzac. As he lived so close to our own time, it might be thought that every biographical detail in regard to so famous a man would be known to this vulgarly inquisitive age; but there are passages in Balzac's life that, despite endless research, are shrouded in baffling obscurity.

However dim and imperfect may be our knowledge of Shakespeare's personal history, one fact stands out clearly in his writings—that he loved "this England" and was a patriot to the core. The greatest of his predecessors in tragedy, short-lived Christopher Marlowe (who was stabbed, 1593, in a tavern-brawl at Deptford in his thirtieth year), had written a fine impressive play on the subject of " Edward II " ; but the popular historical dramas of that time were usually uninspired, mechanical performances. Shakespeare's dramatising of English history is instinct with life and fiery energy. He drew his material chiefly from Holinshed's " Chronicles," 1577, republished with additions in 1587. Sometimes he incorporates in his plays passages of Holinshed with scarcely the change of a word; nor from any old playwright did he scruple to draw whatever hints or suggestions he found useful. Robert Greene, who was a poor dramatist but wrote some beautiful lyrics, considered himself to have been badly treated—robbed of his laurels—by Shakespeare, and bitterly attacked the " upstart crow." The facts are not very clear. Greene was dying when he wrote his notorious invective, and his crazy fancy was doubtless harbouring grievances that were largely imaginary. It is to be noted that Henry Chettle, the editor of Greene's posthumous pamphlet, tendered an apology later to Shakespeare for any offence that might have been given by the dead man's intemperate language. Shakespeare, being himself free from literary vanity, would have little sympathy with smaller writers who were a prey to it. Plays—the best of them—what are they ? In a " Midsummer Night's Dream," Theseus, Duke of Athens, gives us the answer : " The best in this kind are but shadows; and the worst are no worse, if imagination amend them."

The first part of " Henry VI " is the earliest in the series of historical plays, and most critics are agreed that (save for the scene in the Temple Garden in the second act and Suffolk's colloquy with Margaret in the fifth) the passages that can be definitely assigned to Shakespeare are but few. It opens with the funeral of Henry V in Westminster

Abbey, where the great nobles are seen wrangling round the bier. With dramatic suddenness enters a messenger to announce the disasters that have befallen the English arms in France, the capture of town after town. "How were they lost? What treachery was used?" hotly inquires the Duke of Exeter. The messenger's answer is not without significance to-day:

" No treachery; but want of men and money.
    Amongst the soldiers this is muttered,
    That here you maintain several factions;
    And, whilst a field should be despatcht and fought,
    You are disputing of your generals:
    One would have lingering wars, with little cost;
    Another would fly swift, but wanteth wings;
    A third thinks, without expense at all,
    By guileful fair words peace may be obtain'd.
    Awake, awake, English nobility!"

There is much more of Shakespeare's work in the Second and Third Parts of Henry VI than in the First. We are made to realise, with strange vividness, the terrible days of the devastating Wars of the Roses, and our impatience with the pusillanimity of the pious King Henry goes far to blunt our pity for his sufferings and sorrows.

The grim, turbulent tragedy of " Richard III " continues the story from the murder of Henry VI to the battle of Bosworth Field, where the tyrant Richard fell fighting with the desperate courage that never failed him; and the play closes on the note of hope, the union of the White Rose and the Red, the promise of—

" Smooth-faced peace,
    With smiling plenty, and fair prosperous days."

It is curious to note that Shakespeare's contemporary, John Stow, author of the "Annals" and the "Survey of London," who died at eighty in 1605, had talked in his youth with old people who remembered Richard III as "a comely prince." Sir George Buck, whose uncle had fought on Richard's side at Bosworth Field, wrote, in the days of James I, a "History of Richard III," in which he essayed to prove that the murderous usurper had been harshly judged by posterity; and in the eighteenth century Horace Walpole published an exculpatory "Historic Doubts on the Life and Reign of King Richard III," but afterwards recanted. From his portrait Richard would certainly seem to have had (like the infamous Judge Jeffreys, who has been whitewashed in recent years) a remarkably handsome and thoughtful countenance, but no amount of special pleading will persuade us that this ruthless, crafty king is undeserving of the abhorrence in which his memory is popularly held. That just and candid historian, the late James Gairdner, while expressing admiration for Richard's military skill and statesmanlike abilities, makes no attempt to deny or defend his fiendish cruelties.

"Richard II," which probably followed soon after "Richard III" (and may be assigned to 1595-6), bears clear traces of Marlowe's influence, and was also indebted to Samuel Daniel's epic poem, "Civil Wars"; but in John of Gaunt's famous death-speech there is a ringing patriotic fervour that we nowhere find in "mighty" Marlowe or "well-languag'd" Daniel. Hackneyed though it be by constant repetition, that magnificent praise of England never loses its freshness, but from age to age thrills the hearts and souls of her sons at home and oversea :

Shakespeare, the Englishman

" This royal throne of kings, this scepter'd isle,
   This earth of majesty, this seat of Mars,
   This other Eden, demi-Paradise ;
   This fortress built by Nature for herself . . .
   This happy breed of men, this little world ;
   This precious stone set in the silver sea. . . ."

Of late years " Richard II " has seldom been presented on the London stage ; but F. R. Benson,
at the Shakespeare Festival gatherings in Stratford-
on-Avon, has frequently personated Richard with
sympathy and subtlety.

  Nowhere has Shakespeare drawn a more gallant,
loyal, and chivalrous gentleman than Philip Faulconbridge in " King John." The older play, " The
Troublesome Reign of King John " (freely used by
Shakespeare), introduced Faulconbridge, who is
described in it as " A hardy wild-head, tough and
vigorous." This ribald roisterer of the nameless,
forgotten playwright was transformed by Shakespeare's matchless skill into a noble, patriotic soldier
of unconquerable courage, strictest honour, and
infinite tenderness. His memorable words with
which the play closes can never be too often recalled :

" This England never did, nor never shall,
  Lie at the proud foot of a conqueror,
  But when it first did help to wound itself.
  Now these her princes are come home again,
  Come the three corners of the world in arms
  And we shall shock them : naught shall make us rue,
  If England to itself do rest but true."

At the outbreak of the present war many must have
mournfully recalled King John's bewilderment and
indignation when news was brought to him that the
foreign foe had completed with swiftness and
secrecy all his preparations against England—

215

" Oh, where hath our intelligence been drunk ?
Where hath it slept ? "

The two parts of " Henry IV " cover a period of
eleven years—from 1402, the third year of the
aspiring Bolingbroke's reign, to his death in 1413 in
the Jerusalem Chamber at Westminster Abbey.
Written with supreme art—when Shakespeare no
longer needed the guidance of Marlowe—these plays
present in the First Part the strenuous struggles
that the Lancastrian king had to maintain against
powerful and jealous nobles who sought to dispossess
him of the throne he had wrested from the hapless
Richard, and in the Second show the proud conqueror weakened in body, depressed in spirit, and a
prey to remorse for the " indirect crook'd ways "
by which his ambitious end had been achieved. The
spectacle of civil strife, the endless plotting and
counterplotting, would be intolerably painful and
monotonous if Shakespeare's rich, incomparable
humour had not provided the comic relief of Falstaff
and his companions at the Boar's Head in Eastcheap,
and of the delightful pair of country justices, Master
Shallow (with his " good varlet " Davy) and Master
Silence.

Henry V succeeded his father unchallenged,
though the Earl of March (who was devotedly
attached to his supplanter) had a better claim to the
throne. After suppressing a conspiracy of the Earl
of Cambridge, Lord Scroop, and Sir Thomas Grey,
and executing its authors, the King—who has put
away all the madcap levity of his youth and become
a rigid disciplinarian—sails with his slender forces
for France. It is difficult to forgive the great warrior
for his harsh treatment of Falstaff, who evidently
dies of a broken heart, as Nym hints (" the King
hath run bad humours on the knight ; that's the

even of it ") ; yet all is forgotten when we see him
heartening his brothers-in-arms by his dauntless
confidence. Many passages from his speeches have
become part and parcel of our common parlance :
for instance—

" In peace there's nothing so becomes a man
    As modest stillness and humility :
    But when the blast of war blows in our ears,
    Then imitate the action of the tiger ;
    Stiffen the sinews, summon up the blood,
    Disguise fair nature with hard-favour'd rage.

" If we are markt to die, we are enow
    To do our country loss ; and if to live,
    The fewer men, the greater share of honour."

" We few, we happy few, we band of brothers."

" All things are ready if our mind be so."

" Henry VIII," the latest of the historical plays,
deals with the divorce of Katherine of Aragon ; the
fall of Wolsey ; the King's marriage with Katherine's
maid-of-honour, Anne Bullen ; the birth and
christening of the child of the second marriage,
Elizabeth, the future Queen, whose greatness and
glory are predicted at the font (with somewhat
fulsome compliments to her successor James I) in
unctuous and grandiloquent language by Archbishop
Cranmer. Richly staged, " Henry VIII " is still the
delight of playgoers ; but to students the play is a
bone of contention. There can be no doubt that
many scenes were written by Shakespeare's younger
contemporary, John Fletcher ; and it is highly
probable that Fletcher had for collaborator Philip
Massinger. In the very first scene there are (to my
thinking) clear, unmistakable Shakespearean touches ;
the trial-scene of Queen Katherine testifies eloquently to the master's guiding hand ; and, though

Fletcher was at his best in the description of the fall of Wolsey, Shakespeare's revising hand—" the little more, and how much it is ! "—is distinctly traceable. So, too, in other parts of the play ; but I have no space here to discuss the very difficult problems presented by " Henry VIII."

Throughout his " Histories " Shakespeare urgently impresses upon his countrymen the absolute necessity for national unity if England is successfully to resist foreign aggression :—

" O England !—model to thy inward greatness,
　Like little body with a mighty heart,—
　What might'st thou do, that honour would thee do,
　Were all thy children kind and natural ! "
(" Henry V," Act II, Chorus.)

" O, let me have no subject enemies
　When adverse foreigners affright my towns
　With dreadful pomp of stout invasion!"
(" King John," IV, ii.)

Passage after passage might be quoted to show how he detested civil dissensions and exhorted all parties to work together for the common good.

In his Roman tragedies, founded on North's translation (through the French) of Plutarch's " Lives," Shakespeare is often glancing at his own times while he professedly pictures the ancient world. Coleridge styled Shakespeare a " philosophical aristocrat " ; and whatever else may be true or false in regard to our national poet, it may be safely stated that he had a strong dislike of the " many-headed multitude." This comes out clearly enough in " Julius Cæsar " ; but in the later tragedy, " Coriolanus," we are startled by the vehemence of the invective launched by the " gentle Shakespeare " against demagogues and their dupes. We must, it

is true, beware of identifying the views expressed by
particular characters in Shakespeare's plays with the
poet's own personal opinions, but no reader can
resist the conviction that—when he wrote " Coriolanus "—Shakespeare was consumed with indignation
at mean, cowardly politicians who trade in lies and
calumnies, fawning on the populace and traducing
nobler spirits.

A play that bristles with perplexities is " Troilus
and Cressida," which seems to have been written at
various times and certainly—in the form that has
come down—does not give us Shakespeare's " last
hand." It is remarkable for its close-packed wealth
of political wisdom, and without exaggeration one
may say that, for depth and pregnancy, the speeches
of Ulysses have never been surpassed.   But the
language is often difficult and needs close attention
to gather its full import ; hence it is a play that is
very seldom seen on the stage.   Every word of
Ulysses' long admonitory counsel to Achilles (who
in a fit of spleen has doffed his armour and withdrawn sulkily to his tent) is astonishingly cogent :

" Time hath, my lord, a wallet at his back,
   Wherein he puts alms for oblivion,
   A great-sized monster of ingratitudes :
   Those scraps are good deeds past ; which are
      devour'd
   As fast as they are made, forgot as soon
   As done : perseverance, dear my lord,
   Keeps honour bright : to have done, is to hang
   Quite out of fashion, like a rusty mail
   In monumental mockery. Take the instant way ;
   For honour travels in a strait so narrow,
   Where one but goes abreast: keep, then, the path;
   For emulation hath a thousand sons,
   That one by one pursue : if you give way,

Or hedge aside from the direct forthright,
Like to an enter'd tide, they all rush by,
And leave you hindmost. . . ."

Doubtless Shakespeare was thinking of the sleepless
vigilance of that wary and politic statesman Sir
Robert Cecil when he put into Ulysses' mouth the
lines :

" The providence that's in a watchful state
Knows almost every grain of Pluto's gold ;
Finds bottom in th' uncomprehensive deeps ;
Keeps place with thought, and almost, like the gods,
Does thoughts unveil in their dumb cradles . . .
All the commerce that you have had with Troy
As perfectly is ours as yours, my lord."

A play that in tone and temper bears some affinity
to " Troilus and Cressida " is " Timon of Athens."
In satiric pungency, indeed downright savagery,
Shakespeare is here more than a match for Dean
Swift. How " Timon " came to be written we do
not know ; it has descended in a garbled form, and
several scenes were evidently by an inferior hand.

The violent tirades of Timon inevitably remind
us of those terrible, crazed, yet lucid imprecations
of King Lear when he battled his way over the
shelterless heath through the blind fury of the
storm. " Leir, the sonne of Baldud [Bladud]," says
Holinshed, " was admitted ruler over the Britaines
in the yeare of the world 3105, at what time Joas
reigned in Juda." But Shakespeare does not hesitate
to show us a highly developed spy system in that
dim legendary age :

" There is division,
Although as yet the face of it be cover'd
With mutual cunning, 'twixt Albany and Cornwall ;

Who have—as who have not, that their great stars
Throned and set high—servants, who seem no less,
Which are to France the spies and speculations
Intelligent of our State. . . .
But, true it is, from France there comes a power
Into this scatter'd kingdom; who already,
Wise in our negligence, have secret feet
In some of our best ports, and are at point
To show their open banner."

A thousand years go by, and in " Cymbeline "
we are at a time when authentic history and pseudo-
history are interwoven. This rich, romantic play
contains some fine patriotic speeches that one could
wish to hear delivered by worthier speakers than the
wicked Queen and her odious, misshapen son Cloten.
When Caius Lucius comes from Rome to claim the
tribute that had lately been " left untender'd,"
Cloten spiritedly exclaims :

> " Britain is
> A world by itself; and we will nothing pay;
> For wearing our own noses."

Then the Queen makes a stirring appeal to Cymbeline :

> " Remember, sir, my liege,
> The kings your ancestors, together with
> The natural bravery of your isle, which stands
> As Neptune's park, ribbed and paled in
> With rocks unscalable and roaring waters;
> With sands that will not bear your enemies' boats,
> But suck them up to th' topmast. . . ."

Cloten is an irredeemable scoundrel, but for once
we can applaud him when he tersely and pithily
sums up the matter :

"Why tribute? why should we pay tribute?
If Cæsar can hide the sun from us with a blanket,
or put the moon in his pocket, we will pay him
tribute for light: else, sir, no more tribute, pray
you now."

"Cymbeline" is the latest, or nearly the latest, of
Shakespeare's plays : among the earliest is the "Two
Gentlemen of Verona," and there he describes in
lively colours the eager spirit of adventure that
inspired our young men in the years that follow the
defeat of the Spanish Armada. In the opening scene
Valentine is shown taking leave of his friend Proteus :

"Cease to persuade, my loving Proteus :
  Home-keeping youth have ever homely wits.
  Were't not affection chains thy tender days
  To the sweet glances of thy honour'd love,
  I rather would entreat thy company
  To see the wonders of the world abroad,
  Than, living dully sluggardized at home,
  Wear out thy youth with shapeless idleness."

Proteus's uncle chafes at seeing his nephew remain
inactive at home when so many youths are seeking
their fortunes abroad :

Antonio : Tell me, Panthino, what sad talk was that
Wherewith my brother held you in the cloister ?
Panthino : 'Twas of his nephew Proteus, your son.
Antonio : Why, what of him ?
Panthino :   He wonder'd that your lordship
Would suffer him to spend his youth at home
While other men, of slender reputation,
Put forth their sons to seek preferment out :
Some to the wars, to try their fortune there;
Some to discover islands far away ;

222

Some to the studious universities.
For any, or for all these exercises,
He said that Proteus your son was meet;
And did request me to importune you
To let him spend his time no more at home,
Which would be great impeachment to his age,
In having known no travel in his youth."

Though the scene is laid in Italy, Shakespeare was evidently thinking of our English gentlemen-adventurers; and when in " King John " he wrote of—

" Rash, inconsiderate, fiery voluntaries,
    With ladies' faces and fierce dragons' spleens,"

we may be sure that he was describing to the life Elizabethan soldiers of fortune whom he had personally known.

In " A Midsummer Night's Dream " (1595-96; subsequently revised) Shakespeare paid a graceful compliment to Queen Elizabeth (the " fair vestal thronèd in the west ") ; and it is almost certain that the words " the mortal moon hath her eclipse endur'd " in his 107th sonnet allude to the Queen's death. The chorus to the fifth act of " Henry V " has a reference to the expedition of the Earl of Essex in 1599 to Ireland, and tells how eagerly the public was looking forward to his speedy return, " bringing rebellion broachèd on his sword." Essex had been accompanied in his luckless adventure by Shakespeare's early patron, to whom " Venus and Adonis " and " Lucrece " were dedicated, Lord Southampton. Alas ! popular hopes were belied ; the expedition was a failure, and Essex stole back ingloriously, to encounter the wrath of the Queen and her ministers. In desperation this darling of the people attempted to provoke an insurrection ; it was easily suppressed, and, after trial by his peers, he was executed (February 1601). Southampton, who had been implicated in the crazy plot, was committed prisoner to the Tower, where he remained till the accession of James I (1603), by whom he was immediately released. In spite of all his faults of hotheadedness and wrongheadedness, Essex must have possessed most attractive qualities; but his popularity had made him powerful and relentless enemies. Among those who most sedulously and implacably strove to compass his ruin were Sir Walter Raleigh and Sir Francis Bacon; and it was his long-remembered hostility to Essex that in after-times was a powerful factor in making Raleigh (" wily Wat ") so cordially hated. Shakespeare had shown in 1599 a chivalrous admiration for Essex, and we may be sure that his generous pity was stirred by the hapless favourite's fall. It is noteworthy that a play of " Richard II " (doubtless Shakespeare's, though there were other plays on the subject) was acted by Shakespeare's company at the instance of Essex's friends—just before the abortive insurrection —with the object, it was alleged at Essex's trial, of securing popular sympathy for the conspirators.

The sonnet (107) that alludes to the death of Queen Elizabeth seems also to point clearly—in the verse " And peace proclaims olives of endless age " —to her peace-loving successor James I. One of James's peculiarities was that he particularly disliked crowds; and that ill-natured gossip, Arthur Wilson, writes that " in his publick appearances, especially in his sports, the accesses of the people made him so impatient that he often dispersed them with frowns, that we may not say with *curses.*" The commentators have urged, with some plausibility, that Shakespeare may have intended a compliment to King James when he makes the Duke in " Measure for Measure " say—

> "I love the people,
> But do not like to stage me to their eyes:
> Though it do well, I do not relish well
> Their loud applause and aves vehement,
> Not do I think the man of safe discretion
> That does affect it."

James would have been flattered by these words, but he would hardly have relished Lucio's description in Act IV, scene iii—" the old fantastical duke of dark corners." In Act IV of " Macbeth " Shakespeare complimented James in much more definite and unmistakable language.

Shakespeare's plays doubtless contain many political allusions that were readily appreciated by contemporary playgoers but to-day pass undetected. Quite recently (" Modern Philology," vol. xiii, No. 9, January 1916) Mr. T. S. Graves, in a paper on " Pericles," made out a very strong case for his contention that the incident of the grain-ships brought by Pericles in a time of famine to the relief of Tarsus may be connected with James I's allowance (against Cecil's opposition) of the exportation of English grain to the Republic of Venice in 1607. From the Venetian State Papers he shows that the Venetian Ambassador, Zorzi Giustinian, used much patience and diplomatic skill in securing the shipment of this grain to the Republic, that was urgently pressing for it. At the trial of a later Venetian Ambassador, Foscarini, in 1617, it was stated by one of the witnesses, Odoando Guatz, as matter of common knowledge, that " Giustinian went with the French Ambassador and his wife to a play called ' Pericles ' which cost Giustinian more than 20 crowns. He also took the Secretary of Florence." Having successfully carried through this important State-commission, Giustinian would not grudge even

the fairly large sum of twenty crowns in taking
distinguished friends to see a play that introduced
matter so pertinent to his diplomatic triumph.

Such papers as Mr. Graves's are of real interest
and value ; but reckless, irresponsible guesswork has
played far too large a part in Shakespearean study.
One person writes a book to show that Shakespeare
was a Roman Catholic ; another that he was a
zealous Puritan ; a third that he was an atheist.
Hamlet, I have just been reading (and the pro-
pounder of the theory is an old friend of mine), was
Essex. Fiddlesticks ! Seas of ink have been spilled
over the discussion of Shakespeare's Sonnets, but
we are no nearer than ever we were to the heart of
the mystery ; though the silliest commentator of
to-day would hesitate to endorse the view of the
eighteenth-century critic who claimed that they
were addressed to Queen Elizabeth.

On one point we are all agreed—that Shakespeare
is our sovereign poet, the chosen spokesman of the
English race to the nations of the world. Hence
when we read that a learned German professor is
claiming that the sympathy of Shakespeare—the
greatest and most typical of Englishmen in all the
tide of times—would to-day, if he were living, be
with Germany, we are tempted to exclaim with
Touchstone, " God help thee, shallow man ! God
make incision in thee ! thou art raw."